CEN

THE DAILY STUDY BIBLE SERIES
REVISED EDITION

THE LETTERS OF
JOHN AND JUDE

THE LETTERS OF
JOHN
AND
JUDE

REVISED EDITION

Translated
with an Introduction and Interpretation
by
WILLIAM BARCLAY

THE WESTMINSTER PRESS
PHILADELPHIA

Revised Edition
Copyright © 1976 William Barclay

First published by The Saint Andrew Press
Edinburgh, Scotland

I, II, and III John: First Edition, April, 1958
Second Edition, May, 1960

Jude: First Edition, July, 1958
Second Edition, May, 1960

Published by The Westminster Press®
Philadelphia, Pennsylvania

PRINTED IN THE UNITED STATES OF AMERICA

9 8 7 6

TO

MY FRIEND

P. M. S.

A GREAT ENCOURAGER

Library of Congress Cataloging in Publication Data

Bible. N.T. Epistles of John. English. Barclay.
1976.
The Letters of John and Jude.

(The Daily study Bible series. — Rev. ed.)
1. Bible. N.T. Epistles of John — Commentaries.
2. Bible. N.T. Jude — Commentaries. I. Barclay,
William, lecturer in the University of Glasgow.
II. Bible. N.T. Jude. English. Barclay. 1976.
III. Title. IV. Series.
BS2803.B37   1976   227'.94'077   75-37760
ISBN 0-664-21314-6
ISBN 0-664-24114-X pbk.

GENERAL INTRODUCTION

The Daily Study Bible series has always had one aim—to convey the results of scholarship to the ordinary reader. A. S. Peake delighted in the saying that he was a "theological middleman", and I would be happy if the same could be said of me in regard to these volumes. And yet the primary aim of the series has never been academic. It could be summed up in the famous words of Richard of Chichester's prayer—to enable men and women "to know Jesus Christ more clearly, to love him more dearly, and to follow him more nearly".

It is all of twenty years since the first volume of *The Daily Study Bible* was published. The series was the brain-child of the late Rev. Andrew McCosh, M.A., S.T.M., the then Secretary and Manager of the Committee on Publications of the Church of Scotland, and of the late Rev. R. G. Macdonald, O.B.E., M.A., D.D., its Convener.

It is a great joy to me to know that all through the years *The Daily Study Bible* has been used at home and abroad, by minister, by missionary, by student and by layman, and that it has been translated into many different languages. Now, after so many printings, it has become necessary to renew the printer's type and the opportunity has been taken to restyle the books, to correct some errors in the text and to remove some references which have become outdated. At the same time, the Biblical quotations within the text have been changed to use the Revised Standard Version, but my own original translation of the New Testament passages has been retained at the beginning of each daily section.

There is one debt which I would be sadly lacking in courtesy if I did not acknowledge. The work of revision and correction has been done entirely by the Rev. James Martin, M.A., B.D., minister of High Carntyne Church, Glasgow. Had it not been for him this task would never have been undertaken, and it is impossible for me to thank him enough for the selfless toil he has put into the revision of these books.

It is my prayer that God may continue to use *The Daily Study Bible* to enable men better to understand His word.

Glasgow   WILLIAM BARCLAY

CONTENTS

THE LETTERS OF JOHN

INTRODUCTION TO THE
FIRST LETTER OF JOHN

A PERSONAL LETTER AND ITS BACKGROUND

FIRST John is entitled a letter but it has no opening address nor closing greetings such as the letters of Paul have. And yet no one can read it without feeling its intensely personal character. Beyond all doubt the man who wrote it had in his mind's eye a definite situation and a definite group of people. Both the form and the personal character of *First John* will be explained if we think of it as what someone has called "a loving and anxious sermon" written by a pastor who loved his people and sent out to the various churches over which he had charge.

Any such letter is produced by an actual situation apart from which it cannot be fully understood. If, then, we wish to understand *First John* we have first of all to try to reconstruct the situation which produced it, remembering that it was written in Ephesus a little after A.D. 100.

THE FALLING AWAY

By A.D. 100 certain things had almost inevitably happened within the Church, especially in a place like Ephesus.

(i) Many were now second or even third generation Christians. The thrill of the first days had, to some extent at least, passed away. Wordsworth said of one of the great moments of modern history:

> "Bliss was it in that dawn to be alive."

In the first days of Christianity there was a glory and a splendour, but now Christianity had become a thing of habit, "traditional, half-hearted, nominal." Men had grown used to it and something of the wonder was lost. Jesus knew men and he had said: "Most men's love will grow cold" (*Matthew* 24: 12). John was writing at a time when, for some at least, the first thrill was gone and the flame of devotion had died to a flicker.

(ii) One result was that there were members of the Church who found the standards which Christianity demanded a burden and a weariness. They did not want to be *saints* in the New Testament sense of the term. The New Testament word for *saint* is *hagios*, which is also commonly translated *holy*. Its basic meaning is *different*. The Temple was *hagios* because it was *different* from other buildings; the Sabbath was *hagios* because it was *different* from other days; the Jewish nation was *hagios* because it was *different* from other peoples; and the Christian was called to be *hagios* because he was called to be *different* from other men. There was always a distinct cleavage between the Christian and the world. In the Fourth Gospel Jesus says, "If you were of the world, the world would love its own; but because you are not of the world, but I chose you out of the world, therefore the world hates you" (*John* 15: 19). "I have given them thy word," said Jesus in his prayer to God, "and the world has hated them, because they are not of the world, even as I am not of the world" (*John* 17: 14).

All this involved an ethical demand. It demanded a new standard of moral purity, a new kindness, a new service, a new forgiveness—and it was difficult. And once the first thrill and enthusiasm were gone it became harder and harder to stand out against the world and to refuse to conform to the generally accepted standards and practices of the age.

(iii) It is to be noted that *First John* shows no signs that the Church to which it was written was being persecuted. The peril, as it has been put, was not persecution but seduction; it came from within. That, too, Jesus had foreseen. "Many false prophets," he said, "will arise, and lead many astray" (*Matthew* 24: 11). This was a danger of which Paul had warned the leaders of this very Church of Ephesus when he made his farewell address to them. "I know," he said, "that after my departure fierce wolves will come in among you, not sparing the flock. And from among your own selves will arise men, speaking perverse things to draw away the disciples after them" (*Acts* 20: 29, 30).

The trouble which *First John* seeks to combat did not come from men out to destroy the Christian faith but from men who thought they were improving it. It came from men whose aim was to make Christianity intellectually respectable. They knew the intellectual tendencies and currents of the day and felt that the time had come for Christianity to come to terms with secular philosophy and contemporary thought.

THE CONTEMPORARY PHILOSOPHY

What, then, was this contemporary thought and philosophy with which the false prophets and mistaken teachers wished to align the Christian faith? Throughout the Greek world there was a tendency of thought to which the general name of Gnosticism is given. The basic belief of all Gnostic thought was that only spirit was good and matter was essentially evil. The Gnostic, therefore, inevitably despised the world since it was matter. In particular he despised the body which, being matter, was necessarily evil. Imprisoned within this body was the spirit of man. That spirit was a seed of God, who was altogether good. So, then, the aim of life must be to release this heavenly seed imprisoned in the evil of the body. That could be done only by a secret knowledge and elaborate ritual which only the true Gnostic could supply. Here was a tendency of thought which was written deep into Greek thinking—and which has not even yet ceased to exist. Its basis is the conviction that all matter is evil and spirit alone is good, and that the one real aim in life is to liberate man's spirit from the vile prison-house of the body.

THE FALSE TEACHERS

With that in our minds let us turn to *First John* and gather the evidence as to who these false teachers were and what they taught. They had been within the Church but they had seceded from it. "They went out from us, but they were not of us" (1 *John* 2: 19). They were men of influence for they claimed to be prophets. "Many false prophets have gone out into the world" (1 *John* 4: 1). Although they had left the

Church, they still tried to disseminate their teaching within it and to seduce its members from the true faith (1 *John* 2: 26).

THE DENIAL OF JESUS'S MESSIAHSHIP

At least some of these false teachers denied that Jesus was the Messiah. "Who is a liar," demands John, "but he who denies that Jesus is the Christ?" (1 *John* 2: 22). It is most likely that these false teachers were not Gnostics proper, but Jews. Things had always been difficult for Jewish Christians, but the events of history made them doubly so. It was very difficult for a Jew to come to believe in a crucified Messiah. But suppose he had begun so to believe, his difficulties were by no means finished. The Christians believed that Jesus would return quickly to vindicate his people. Clearly that would be a hope that would be specially dear to the heart of the Jews. Then in A.D. 70 Jerusalem was captured by the Romans, who were so infuriated with the long intransigence and the suicidal resistance of the Jews that they tore the Holy City stone from stone and drew a plough across the midst of it. In view of that, how could any Jew easily accept the hope that Jesus would come and save his people? The Holy City was desolate; the Jews were dispersed throughout the world. In face of that how could it be true that the Messiah had come?

THE DENIAL OF THE INCARNATION

There was something even more serious than that. There was false teaching which came directly from an attempt from within the Church to bring Christianity into line with Gnosticism. We must remember the Gnostic point of view that spirit alone was good and matter utterly evil. *Given that point of view any real incarnation is impossible.* That is exactly what centuries later Augustine was to point out. Before he became a Christian, he was skilled in the philosophies of the various schools. In the *Confessions* (6: 9) he tells us that somewhere in the heathen writers he had read in one form or another nearly all the things which Christianity says; but there was one great Christian saying which he had never found in any pagan author and which no one would ever find, and that saying was: "The Word became flesh and dwelt among us" (*John* 1: 14). Since the heathen thinkers believed in the essential evil of matter and therefore the essential evil of the body, that was one thing they could never say.

It is clear that the false teachers against whom John was writing in this First Letter denied the reality of the incarnation and of Jesus's physical body. "Every spirit," writes John, "which confesses that Jesus Christ has come in the flesh is of God; and every spirit which does not confess Jesus is not of God" (1 *John* 4: 2, 3).

In the early Church this refusal to admit the reality of the incarnation took, broadly speaking, two forms.

(i) In its most radical and wholesale form it was called *Docetism*, which Goodspeed suggests might be translated *Seemism*. The Greek verb *dokein* means *to seem*; and the Docetists taught that Jesus only *seemed* to have a body. They insisted that he was a purely spiritual being who had nothing but the appearance of having a body. One of the apocryphal books written from this point of view is the *Acts of John*, which dates from about A.D. 160. In it John is made to say that sometimes when he touched Jesus he seemed to meet with a material body but at other times "the substance was immaterial, as if it did not exist at all," and also that when Jesus walked he never left any footprint upon the ground. The simplest form of Docetism is the complete denial that Jesus ever had a physical body.

(ii) There was a more subtle, and perhaps more dangerous, variant of this theory connected with the name of Cerinthus. In tradition John and Cerinthus were sworn enemies. Eusebius (*Ecclesiastical History* 4: 14.6) hands down a story which tells how John went to the public bathhouse in Ephesus to bathe. He saw Cerinthus inside and refused even to enter the building. "Let us flee," he said, "lest even the bathhouse fall, because Cerinthus the enemy of truth is within." Cerinthus drew a definite distinction between the human Jesus and the divine Christ. He said that Jesus was a man, born in a perfectly natural way. He lived in special obedience to God, and after his baptism the Christ in the shape of a dove descended upon him, from that power which is above all powers, and then he brought to men news of the Father who had been as yet unknown. Cerinthus did not stop there. He said that at the end of Jesus's life, the Christ again withdrew from him so that the Christ never suffered at all. It was the human Jesus who suffered, died and rose again.

This again comes out in the stories of the apocryphal gospels written under the influence of this point of view. In the *Gospel of Peter*, written about A.D. 130, it is said that Jesus showed no pain upon the Cross and that his cry was: "My power! My power! Why hast thou forsaken me?" It was at that moment that the divine Christ left the human Jesus. The *Acts of John* go further. They tell how, when the human Jesus was being crucified on Calvary, John was actually talking to the divine Christ in a cave in the hillside and that the Christ said to him, "John, to the multitude down below in Jerusalem I am being crucified, and pierced with lances and with reeds, and gall and vinegar are given me to drink. But I am speaking to you, and listen to what I say. . . . Nothing, therefore, of the things they will say of me have I suffered" (*Acts of John* 97).

We may see how widespread this way of thinking was from the Letters of Ignatius. He was writing to a group of Churches in Asia Minor which must have been much the same as that to which *First John* was written. When Ignatius wrote he was a prisoner and was being conveyed to Rome to be martyred by being flung to the beasts in the arena. He wrote to the Trallians: "Be deaf, therefore, when anyone speaks to you apart from Jesus Christ, who was of the family of David and Mary, who was truly born, both ate and drank, was truly persecuted under Pontius Pilate, was truly crucified and died . . . who also was truly raised from the dead. . . . But if, as some affirm, who are without God—that is, who are unbelievers— his suffering was only a semblance . . . why am I a prisoner?" (Ignatius: *To the Trallians* 9 and 10). To the Christians at

Smyrna he wrote: "For he suffered all these things for us that we might attain salvation, and he truly suffered even as he also truly raised himself, not as some unbelievers say that his passion was merely in semblance" (*To the Smyrnaeans* 2). Polycarp writing to the Philippians used John's very words: "For everyone who does not confess that Jesus Christ has come in the flesh is an anti-Christ" (*To the Philippians* 7: 1).

This teaching of Cerinthus is also rebuked in *First John*. John writes of Jesus: "This is he who came by water and blood, Jesus Christ; *not with the water only, but with the water and the blood*" (1 *John* 5: 6). The point of that verse is that the Gnostic teachers would have agreed that the divine Christ came by *water*, that is, at the baptism of Jesus; but they would have denied that he came by *blood*, that is, by the Cross, for they insisted that the divine Christ left the human Jesus before his crucifixion.

The great danger of this heresy is that it comes from what can only be called a mistaken reverence. It is afraid to ascribe to Jesus full humanity. It regards it as irreverent to think that he had a truly physical body. It is a heresy which is by no means dead but is held to this day, usually quite unconsciously, by not a few devout Christians. But it must be remembered, as John so clearly saw, that man's salvation was dependent on the full identification of Jesus Christ with him. As one of the great early fathers unforgettably put it: "He became what we are to make us what he is."

(iii) This Gnostic belief had certain practical consequences in the lives of those who held it.

(*a*) The Gnostic attitude to matter and to all created things produced a certain attitude to the body and the things of the body. That attitude might take any one of three different forms.

(1) It might take the form of asceticism, with fasting and celibacy and rigid control, even deliberate ill-treatment, of the body. The view that celibacy is better than marriage and that sex is sin go back to Gnostic influence and belief— and this is a view which still lingers on in certain quarters.

There is no trace of that view in this letter.

(2) It might take the form of a contention that the body did not matter and that, therefore, its appetites might be gratified without limit. Since the body was in any event evil, it made no difference what a man did with it. There are echoes of this in this letter. John condemns as a liar the man who says that he knows God and yet does not keep God's commandments; the man who says that he abides in Christ ought to walk as Christ walked (1 *John* 1: 6; 2: 4–6). There were clearly Gnostics in these communities who claimed special knowledge of God but whose conduct was far removed from the demand of the Christian ethic.

In certain quarters this Gnostic belief went even further. The Gnostic was the man who had *gnōsis, knowledge*. Some held that the real Gnostic must, therefore, know the best as well as the worst and must enter into every experience of life at its highest or at its deepest level, as the case may be. It might almost be said that such men held that it was an obligation to sin. There is a reference to this kind of belief in the letter to Thyatira in the *Revelation*, where the Risen Christ refers to those who have known "the deep things of Satan" (*Revelation* 2: 24). And it may well be that John is referring to these people when he insists that "God is light, and in him is no darkness at all" (1 *John* 1: 5). These particular Gnostics would have held that there was in God not only blazing light but deep darkness—and that a man must penetrate both. It is easy to see the disastrous consequences of such a belief.

(3) There was a third kind of Gnostic belief. The true Gnostic regarded himself as an altogether spiritual man, as having shed all the material things of life and released his spirit from the bondage of matter. Such Gnostics held that they were so spiritual that they were above and beyond sin and had reached spiritual perfection. It is to them that John refers when he speaks of those who deceive themselves by saying that they have no sin (1 *John* 1: 8–10).

Whichever of these three ways Gnostic belief took, its ethical consequences were perilous in the extreme; and it is clear that its last two were to be found in the society to which John wrote.

(b) Further, this Gnosticism issued in an attitude to men which was the necessary destruction of Christian fellowship. We have seen that the Gnostic aimed at the release of the spirit from the prison house of the evil body by means of an elaborate and esoteric knowledge. Clearly such a knowledge was not for every man. Ordinary people were too involved in the everyday life and work of the world ever to have time for the study and discipline necessary; and, even if they had had such time, many were intellectually incapable of grasping the involved speculations of Gnostic theosophy and philosophy so-called.

This produced an inevitable result. It divided men into two classes—those who were capable of a really spiritual life and those who were not. The Gnostics had names for these two classes of men. The ancients commonly divided the being of man into three parts. There was the *sōma*, the *body*, the physical part of man. There was the *psuchē*, which we generally translate *soul*, but we must have a care for it does not mean what we mean by soul. To the Greeks the *psuchē* was the principle of physical life. Everything which had physical life had *psuchē*. *Psuchē* was that life principle which a man shared with all living creatures. There was the *pneuma*, the spirit; and it was the spirit which was possessed only by man and made him kin to God.

The aim of Gnosticism was the release of the *pneuma* from the *sōma*; but that release could be won only by long and arduous study which only the leisured intellectual could ever undertake. The Gnostics, therefore, divided men into two classes—the *psuchikoi*, who could never advance beyond the principle of physical life and never attain to anything else than what was to all intents and purposes animal living; and the *pneumatikoi*, who were truly spiritual and truly akin to God.

The result was clear. The Gnostics produced a spiritual

aristocracy who looked with contempt and even hatred on lesser men. The *pneumatikoi* regarded the *psuchikoi* as contemptible, earthbound creatures who could never know what real religion was. The consequence was obviously the annihilation of Christian fellowship. That is why John insists all over his letter that the true test of Christianity is love for the brethren. If we really are walking in the light we have fellowship with one another (1: 7). He who says he is in the light and hates his brother is in fact in darkness (2: 9–11). The proof that we have passed from dark to light is that we love the brethren (3: 14–17). The marks of Christianity are belief in Christ and love for the brethren (3: 23). God is love and he who does not love does not know God at all (4: 7, 8). Because God loved us, we ought to love each other; it is when we love each other that God dwells in us (4: 10–12). The commandment is that he who loves God must love his brother also, and he who says he loves God and at the same time hates his brother is branded as a liar (4: 20, 21). The Gnostic, to put it bluntly, would have said that the mark of true religion is contempt for ordinary men; John insists in every chapter that the mark of true religion is love for every man.

Here, then, is a picture of these Gnostic heretics. They talked of being born of God, of walking in the light, of having no sin, of dwelling in God, of knowing God. These were their catch phrases. They had no idea of destroying the Church and the faith; by their way of it they were going to cleanse the Church of dead wood and make Christianity an intellectually respectable philosophy, fit to stand beside the great systems of the day. But the effect of their teaching was to deny the incarnation, to eliminate the Christian ethic and to make fellowship within the Church impossible. It is little wonder that John seeks, with such fervent pastoral devotion, to defend the churches he loved from such an insidious attack from within. This was a threat far more perilous than any heathen persecution; the very existence of the Christian faith was at stake.

THE MESSAGE OF JOHN

First John is a short letter and we cannot look within it for a systematic exposition of the Christian faith. None the less it will be of the greatest interest to examine the basic underlying beliefs with which John confronts those threatening to be the wreckers of the Christian faith.

THE OBJECT OF WRITING

John's object in writing is two-fold yet one. He writes that the joy of his people may be complete (1: 4), and that they may not sin (2: 1). He sees clearly that, however attractive the wrong way may be, it is not in its nature to bring happiness. To bring them joy and to preserve them from sin is one and the same thing.

THE IDEA OF GOD

John has two great things to say about God. God is light and in him there is no darkness at all (1: 5). God is love and that made him love us before we loved him and made him send his son as a remedy for our sins (4: 7–10, 16). John's conviction is that God is self-revealing and self-giving. He is light, and not darkness; he is love, and not hate.

THE IDEA OF JESUS

Because the main attack of the false teachers was on the person of Christ, this letter, which is concerned to answer them, is specially rich and helpful in what it has to say about him.

(i) Jesus is he who was from the beginning (1: 1; 2: 14). When a man is confronted with Jesus, he is confronted with the eternal.

(ii) Another way of putting this is to say that Jesus is the Son of God and for John it is essential to be convinced of that (4: 15; 5: 5). The relationship of Jesus to God is unique and in him is seen God's ever-seeking and ever-forgiving heart.

(iii) Jesus is the Christ, the Messiah (2: 22; 5: 1). That again for him is an essential article of belief. It may seem that here we come into a region of ideas which is much narrower and, in fact, specifically Jewish. But there is something essential here. To say that Jesus is from the beginning and that he is the Son of God is to conserve his connection with *eternity*; to say that he is the Messiah, is to conserve his connection with *history*. It is to see his coming as the event towards which God's plan, working itself out in his chosen people, was moving.

(iv) Jesus was most truly and fully man. To deny that Jesus came in the flesh is to be moved by the spirit of Antichrist (4: 2, 3). It is John's witness that Jesus was so truly man that he himself had known and touched and handled him (1: 1, 3). No writer in the New Testament holds with greater intensity the full reality of the incarnation. Not only did he become man, he also suffered for men. It was by water and blood that he came (5: 6); and he laid down his life for men (3: 16).

(v) The coming of Jesus, his incarnation, his life, his death, his resurrection and his ascension all combine to deal with the sin of man. Jesus was without sin (3: 5); and man is essentially a sinner, even though in his arrogance he may claim to be without sin (1: 8–10); and yet the sinless one came to take away the sin of sinning men (3: 5). In regard to man's sin Jesus is two things.

(*a*) He is our *advocate* with the Father (2: 1). The word is *paraklētos*. A *paraklētos* is someone who is called in to help. The word could be used of a doctor; it was often used of a witness called in to give evidence in favour of someone on trial or of a defending lawyer called in to defend someone under accusation. Jesus pleads our case with God; he, the sinless one, is the defender of sinning men.

(*b*) But Jesus is more than that. Twice John calls him the *expiation* for our sins (2: 2; 4: 10). When a man sins, the relationship which should exist between him and God is broken. An expiatory sacrifice is one which restores that relationship or, rather, a sacrifice in virtue of which that relationship is restored. It is an *atoning* sacrifice, a sacrifice which once again makes man and God *at one*. So, then, through what Jesus was and did the relationship between God and man, broken by sin, is restored. Jesus does not only plead the case of the sinner; he sets him at one, with God. The blood of Jesus Christ cleanses us from all sin (1: 7).

(vi) In consequence of all this, through Jesus Christ men who believe have life (4: 9; 5: 11, 12). This is true in a double sense. They have life in the sense that they are saved from death; and they have life in the sense that living has ceased to be mere existence and has become life indeed.

(vii) All this may be summed up by saying that Jesus is the Saviour of the world (4: 14). Here we have something which has to be set out in full. "The Father sent the Son to be the Saviour of the world" (4: 14). We have already talked of Jesus as pleading men's case before God. If we were to leave that without addition, it might be argued that God wished to condemn men and was deflected from his dire purpose by the self-sacrifice of Jesus Christ. But that is not so because for John, as for every writer in the New Testament, the whole initiative was with God. It was he who sent his son to be the Saviour of men.

Within the short compass of this letter the wonder and the glory and the grace of Christ are most fully set out.

THE SPIRIT

In this letter John has less to say about the Spirit; for his highest teaching about him we must turn back to the Fourth Gospel. It may be said that in *First John* the function of the Spirit is in some sense to be the liaison between God and man. It is he who makes us conscious that there is within us the abiding presence of God through Jesus Christ (3: 24; 4: 13). We may say that it is the Spirit who enables us to grasp the precious fellowship with God which is being offered to us.

THE WORLD

The world within which the Christian lives is hostile; it is a world without God. It does not know the Christian, because it did not know Christ (3: 1). It hates the Christian, just as it hated Christ (3: 13). The false teachers are of the world and not of God, and it is because they speak its language that the world is ready to hear them and accept them (4: 4, 5). The whole world, says John sweepingly, is in the power of the evil one (5: 19). It is for that reason that the Christian has to overcome it, and his weapon in his struggle with the world is faith (5: 4).

Hostile as the world is, it is doomed. The world and all its desires are passing away (2: 17). That, indeed, is why it is folly to give one's heart to the world; it is on the way to dissolution. Although the Christian lives in a hostile world which is passing away, there is no need for despair and fear. The darkness is past, the true light now shines (2: 8). God in Christ has broken into time; the new age has come. It is not yet fully realized but the consummation is sure.

The Christian lives in an evil and a hostile world, but he possesses that by which he can overcome it and, when the destined end of the world comes, he is safe, because he already possesses that which makes him a member of the new community in the new age.

THE FELLOWSHIP OF THE CHURCH

John does more than move in the high realms of theology; he has certain most practical things to say about the Christian Church and the Christian life. No New Testament writer stresses more consistently or more strenuously the necessity of Christian fellowship. Christians, John was convinced, are not only bound to God, they are also bound to each other. When we walk in the light, we have fellowship with each other (1: 7). The man who claims to walk in the light but hates his brother, is in reality walking in darkness; it is the man who loves his brother who is in the light (2: 9–11). The proof that a man has passed from darkness to light is the fact that he loves his brother. To hate one's brother man is in essence to be a murderer, as Cain was. If any man is able out of his fullness to help his brother's poverty and does not do so, it is ridiculous for him to claim that the love of God dwells in him. The essence of religion is to believe on the name of the Lord Jesus Christ and to love one another (3: 11–17, 23). God is love; and, therefore, the man who loves is kin to God. God has loved us, and that is the best reason for loving each other (4: 7–12). If a man says that he loves God and at the same time hates his brother, he is a liar. The command is that he who loves God must love his brother also (4: 20, 21).

It was John's conviction that the only way in which a man can prove that he loves God is by loving his fellow-men; and that that love must be not only a sentimental emotion but a dynamic towards practical help.

THE RIGHTEOUSNESS OF THE CHRISTIAN

No New Testament writer makes a stronger ethical demand than John, or more strongly condemns a so-called religion which fails to issue in ethical action. God is righteous and the life of every one who knows him must reflect his righteousness (2: 29). Whoever abides in Christ and is born of God, does not sin; whoever does not do right is not of God (3: 3–10); and the characteristic of this righteousness is that it issues in love for the brethren (3: 10, 11). We show our love to God and to men by keeping God's commandments (5: 2). Whoever is born of God does not sin (5: 18).

For John, knowledge of God and obedience to him must ever go hand in hand. It is by keeping his commandments that we prove that we really do know God. The man who says that he knows him and who does not keep his commandments is a liar (2: 3–5).

It is, in fact, this obedience which is the basis of effective prayer. We receive what we ask of God because we keep his commandments and do what is pleasing in his sight (3: 22).

The two marks which characterize genuine Christianity are

love of the brethren and obedience to the revealed commandments of God.

THE DESTINATION OF THE LETTER

There are certain baffling problems in regard to the letter's destination. The letter itself gives us no clue as to where it was sent. Tradition strongly connects it with Asia Minor, and especially with Ephesus, where, according to tradition, John lived for many years. But there are certain other odd facts which somehow have to be explained.

Cassiodorus says that the First Letter of John was written *Ad Parthos*, To the Parthians; and Augustine has a series of ten tractates written on The Epistle of John *ad Parthos*. One Geneva manuscript still further complicates the matter by entitling the letter *Ad Sparthos*. There is no such word as *Sparthos*. There are two possible explanations of this impossible title. (i) Just possibly it is meant for *Ad Sparsos*, which would mean To the Christians scattered abroad; (ii) In Greek *Ad Parthos* would be *Pros Parthous*. Now in the early manuscripts there was no space between the words and they were all written in capital letters so that the title would run PROSPARTHOUS. A scribe writing to dictation could quite easily put that down as PROSSPARTHOUS, especially if he did not know what the title meant. *Ad Sparthos* can be eliminated as a mere mistake.

But where did To the Parthians come from? There is one possible explanation. *Second John* does tell us of its destination; it is written to *The elect lady and her children* (2 *John* 1). Let us turn to the end of *First Peter*. The Authorized Version has: "The church that is at Babylon, elected together with you, saluteth you" (1 *Peter* 5: 13). The phrase *the church that is* is printed in the Authorized Version in italics which of course, means that it has no equivalent in the Greek which has, in fact, no actual mention of a *church* at all. This the Revised Standard Version accurately indicates: "She who is at Babylon, who is likewise chosen (elect), sends you greetings." As far as the Greek goes it would be perfectly possible, and

indeed natural, to take that as referring not to a *Church* but
to a *lady*. That is precisely what certain of the scholars in the
very early Church did. Now we get *the elect lady* again in
Second John. It was easy to identify the two elect ladies
and to assume that *Second John* was also written to Babylon.
The natural title for the inhabitants of Babylon was Parthians
and hence we have the explanation of the title.

The process went even further. The Greek for *the elect lady*
is *hē elektē*. We have already seen that the early manuscripts
were written all in capital letters; and it would be just possible
to take *Elektē* not as an adjective meaning *elect* but as a
proper name, *Elekta*. This is, in fact, what Clement of
Alexandria may have done, for we have information that he
said that the Johannine letters were written to a certain
Babylonian lady, Elekta by name, and to her children.

It may well be then, that the title *Ad Parthos* arose from a
series of misunderstandings. *The elect one* in *First Peter* is quite
certainly the church, as the Authorized Version rightly saw.
Moffatt translates: "Your sister church in Babylon, elect like
yourselves, salutes you." Further, it is almost certain that in
any event *Babylon* there stands for *Rome* which the early
writers identified with Babylon, the great harlot, drunk with
the blood of the saints (cp. *Revelation* 17: 5). The title *Ad
Parthos* has a most interesting history but clearly it arose from
an ingenious misunderstanding.

There is one further complication. Clement of Alexandria
referred to John's letters as "written to virgins." On the
face of it that is improbable, for it would not be a specially
relevant title for them. How, then, could it come about? The
Greek would be *Pros Parthenous* which closely resembles
Pros Parthous; and, it so happens, John was regularly called
Ho Parthenos, the Virgin, because he never married and
because of the purity of his life. This further title must have
come from a confusion between *Ad Parthos* and *Ho Parthenos*.

This is a case where we may take it that tradition is right
and all the ingenious theories mistaken. We may take it that
these letters were written in Ephesus and to the surrounding

Churches in Asia Minor. When John wrote, it would certainly be to the district where his writ ran, and that was Ephesus and the surrounding territory. He is never mentioned in connection with Babylon.

IN DEFENCE OF THE FAITH

John wrote his great letter to meet a threatening situation and in defence of the faith. The heresies which he attacked are by no means altogether echoes of "old unhappy far off things and battles long ago." They are still beneath the surface and sometimes they even still raise their heads. To study his letter will confirm us in the true faith and enable us to have a defence against that which would seduce us from it.

1 JOHN

THE PASTOR'S AIM

1 *John* 1 : 1–4

> What we are telling you about is that which was from the beginning, that which we heard, that which we saw with our eyes, that which we gazed upon, and which our hands touched. It is about the word of life that we are telling you. (And the life appeared to us, and we saw it, and testify to it; and we are now bringing you the message of this eternal life, which was with the Father and which appeared to us). It is about what we saw and heard that we are bringing the message to you, that you too may have fellowship with us, for our fellowship is with the Father and with Jesus Christ, the Son. And we are writing these things to you that your joy may be completed.

EVERY man, when he sits down to write a letter or rises to preach a sermon, has some object in view. He wishes to produce some effect in the minds and hearts and lives of those to whom his message is addressed. And here at the very beginning of his letter John sets down his objects in writing to his people.

(i) It is his wish to produce fellowship with men and fellowship with God (verse 3). The pastor's aim must always be to bring men closer to one another and closer to God. Any message which is productive of division is a false message. The Christian message can be summed up as having two great aims—love for men and love for God.

(ii) It is his wish to bring his people joy (verse 4). Joy is the essence of Christianity. A message whose only effect is to depress and to discourage those who hear it has stopped halfway. It is quite true that often the aim of the preacher and the teacher must be to awaken a godly sorrow which will lead to a true repentance. But after the sense of sin has been produced, men must be led to the Saviour in whom sins are all forgiven. The ultimate note of the Christian message is joy.

(iii) To that end his aim is to set Jesus Christ before them. A great teacher always used to tell his students that their one aim as preachers must be "to speak a good word for Jesus Christ"; and it was said of another great saint that wherever his conversation began it cut straight across country to Jesus Christ.

The simple fact is that if men are ever to find fellowship with one another and fellowship with God, and if they are ever to find true joy, they must find them in Jesus Christ.

THE PASTOR'S RIGHT TO SPEAK

1 *John* 1: 1–4 (*continued*)

HERE at the very beginning of his letter John sets down his right to speak; and it consists in one thing—in personal experience of Christ (verses 2 and 3).

(i) He says that he has *heard* Christ. Long ago Zedekiah had said to Jeremiah: "Is there any word from the Lord?" (*Jeremiah* 37: 17). What men are interested in is not someone's opinions and guesses but a word from the Lord. It was said of one great preacher that first he listened to God and then he spoke to men; and it was said of John Brown of Haddington that, when he preached, he paused ever and again, as if listening for a voice. The true teacher is the man who has a message from Jesus Christ because he has heard his voice.

(ii) He says that he has *seen* Christ. It is told of Alexander Whyte, the great Scottish preacher, that someone once said to him, "You preached today as if you had come straight from the presence." And Whyte answered, "Perhaps I did." We cannot see Christ in the flesh as John did; but we can still see him with the eye of faith.

> "And, warm, sweet, tender, even yet
> A present help is he;
> And faith has still its Olivet,
> And love its Galilee."

(iii) He says that he has *gazed* on Christ. What, then, is the difference between *seeing* Christ and *gazing* upon him? In the Greek the verb for *to see* is *horan* and it means simply to see with physical sight. The verb for *to gaze* is *theasthai* and it means to gaze at someone or something until something has been grasped of the significance of that person or thing. So Jesus, speaking to the crowds of John the Baptist, asked: "What did you go out into the wilderness *to see* (*theasthai*)?" (*Luke* 7: 24); and in that word he describes how the crowds flocked out to gaze at John and wonder who and what this man might be. Speaking of Jesus in the prologue to his gospel, John says, "We beheld his glory" (*John* 1: 14). The verb is again *theasthai* and the idea is not that of a passing glance but of a steadfast searching gaze which seeks to discover something of the mystery of Christ.

(iv) He says that his hands actually *touched* Christ. Luke tells of how Jesus came back to his disciples, when he had risen from the dead, and said, "See my hands and my feet, that it is I myself: handle me and see, for a spirit has not flesh and bones as you see that I have" (*Luke* 24: 39). Here John is thinking of those people called the Docetists who were so spiritually-minded that they insisted that Jesus never at any time had a flesh and blood body but was only a phantom in human form. They refused to believe that God could ever soil himself by taking human flesh and blood upon himself. John here insists that the Jesus he had known was, in truth, a man amongst men; he felt there was nothing in all the world more dangerous—as we shall see—than to doubt that Jesus was fully man.

THE PASTOR'S MESSAGE

1 *John* 1: 1–4 (*continued*)

JOHN's message is of Jesus Christ; and of Jesus he has three great things to say. First, he says that Jesus was *from the beginning*. That is to say, in him eternity entered time; in him the eternal God personally entered the world of men. Second, that entry into the world of men was a real entry, it was real manhood that God took upon himself. Third, through that action there came to men the word of life, the word which can change death into life and mere existence into real living. Again and again in the New Testament the gospel is called a word; and it is of the greatest interest to see the various connections in which this term is used.

(i) Oftener than anything else the gospel message is called the *word of God* (*Acts* 4: 31; 6: 2, 7; 11: 1; 13: 5, 7, 44; 16: 32; *Philippians* 1: 14; 1 *Thessalonians* 2: 13; *Hebrews* 13: 7; *Revelation* 1: 2, 9; 6: 9; 20: 4). It is not a human discovery; it comes from God. It is news of God which man could not have discovered for himself.

(ii) Frequently the gospel message is called the *word of the Lord* (*Acts* 8: 25; 12: 24; 13: 49; 15: 35; 1 *Thessalonians* 1: 8; 2 *Thessalonians* 3: 1). It is not always certain whether the Lord is God or Jesus, but more often than not it is Jesus who is meant. The gospel is, therefore, the message which God could have sent to men in no other way than through his son.

(iii) Twice the gospel message is called the *word of hearing* (*logos akoēs*) (1 *Thessalonians* 2: 13; *Hebrews* 4: 2). That is to say, it depends on two things, on a voice ready to speak it and an ear ready to hear it.

(iv) The gospel message is the *word of the Kingdom* (*Matthew* 13: 19). It is the announcement of the kingship of God and the summons to render to God the obedience which will make a man a citizen of that kingdom.

(v) The gospel message is the *word of the gospel* (*Acts* 15: 7; *Colossians* 1: 5). *Gospel* means *good news*; and the gospel is essentially good news to man about God.

(vi) The gospel is the *word of grace* (*Acts* 14: 3; 20: 32). It is the good news of God's generous and undeserved love for man; it is the news that man is not saddled with the impossible task of earning God's love but is freely offered it.

(vii) The gospel is the *word of salvation* (*Acts* 13: 26). It is the offer of forgiveness for past sin and of power to overcome sin in the future.

(viii) The gospel is the *word of reconciliation* (2 *Corinthians* 5: 19). It is the message that the lost relationship between man and God is restored in Jesus Christ who has broken down the barrier between man and God which sin had erected.

(ix) The gospel is the *word of the Cross* (1 *Corinthians* 1: 18). At the heart of the gospel is the Cross on which is shown to man the final proof of the forgiving, sacrificing, seeking love of God.

(x) The gospel is the *word of truth* (2 *Corinthians* 6: 7; *Ephesians* 1: 13; *Colossians* 1: 5; 2 *Timothy* 2: 15). With the coming of the gospel it is no longer necessary to guess and grope for Jesus Christ has brought to us the truth about God.

(xi) The gospel is the *word of righteousness* (*Hebrews* 5: 13). It is by the power of the gospel that a man is enabled to break from the power of evil and to rise to the righteousness which is pleasing in the sight of God.

(xii) The gospel is *the health-giving word* (2 *Timothy* 1: 13; 2: 8). It is the antidote which cures the poison of sin and the medicine which defeats the disease of evil.

(xiii) The gospel is the *word of life* (*Philippians* 2: 16). It is through its power that a man is delivered from death and enabled to enter into life at its best.

GOD IS LIGHT

1 *John* 1: 5

> And this is the message which we have heard from him, and which we pass on to you, that God is light, and there is no darkness in him.

A MAN'S own character will necessarily be determined by the character of the god whom he worships; and, therefore, John begins by laying down the nature of the God and Father of Jesus Christ whom Christians worship. God, he says, is light, and there is no darkness in him. What does this statement tell us about God?

(i) It tells us that he is splendour and glory. There is nothing so glorious as a blaze of light piercing the darkness. To say that God is light tells us of his sheer splendour.

(ii) It tells us that God is self-revealing. Above all things light is seen; and it illumines the darkness round about it. To say that God is light is to say that there is nothing secretive or furtive about him. He wishes to be seen and to be known by men.

(iii) It tells us of God's purity and holiness. There is none of the darkness which cloaks hidden evil in God. That he is light speaks to us of his white purity and stainless holiness.

(iv) It tells us of the guidance of God. It is one of the great functions of light to show the way. The road that is lit is the road that is plain. To say that God is light is to say that he offers his guidance for the footsteps of men.

(v) It tells us of the revealing quality in the presence of God. Light is the great revealer. Flaws and stains which are hidden in the shade are obvious in the light. Light reveals the imperfections in any piece of workmanship or material. So the imperfections of life are seen in the presence of God. Whittier wrote:

> "Our thoughts lie open to thy sight;
>   And naked to thy glance;
>   Our secret sins are in the light
>   Of thy pure countenance."

We can never know either the depth to which life has fallen or the height to which it may rise until we see it in the revealing light of God.

THE HOSTILE DARK

1 *John* 1 : 5 (*continued*)

IN God, says John, there is no darkness at all. Throughout the New Testament darkness stands for the very opposite of the Christian life.

(i) Darkness stands for the Christless life. It represents the life that a man lived before he met Christ or the life that he lives if he strays away from him. John writes to his people that, now that Christ has come, the darkness is past and the true light shines (1 *John* 2: 8). Paul writes to his Christian friends that once they were darkness but now they are light in the Lord (*Ephesians* 5: 8). God has delivered us from the power of darkness and brought us into the Kingdom of his dear Son (*Colossians* 1: 13). Christians are not in darkness, for they are children of the day (1 *Thessalonians* 5: 4, 5). Those who follow Christ shall not walk in darkness, as others must, but they will have the light of life (*John* 8: 12). God has called the Christians out of darkness into his marvellous light (1 *Peter* 2: 9).

(ii) The dark is hostile to the light. In the prologue to his gospel John writes that the light shines in the darkness, and the darkness has not overcome it (*John* 1: 5). It is a picture of the darkness seeking to obliterate the light—but unable to overpower it. The dark and the light are natural enemies.

(iii) The darkness stands for the ignorance of life apart from Christ. Jesus summons his friends to walk in the light lest the darkness come upon them, for the man who walks in the darkness does not know where he is going (*John* 12: 35). Jesus is the light, and he has come that those who believe in him should not walk in darkness (*John* 12: 46). The dark stands for the essential lostness of life without Christ.

(iv) The darkness stands for the chaos of life without God. God, says Paul, thinking of the first act of creation, commanded his light to shine out of the darkness (2 *Corinthians* 4: 6). Without God's light the world is a chaos, in which life has neither order nor sense.

(v) The darkness stands for the immorality of the Christless life. It is Paul's appeal to men that they should cast off the works of darkness (*Romans* 13: 12). Men, because their deeds were evil, loved the darkness rather than the light (*John* 3: 19). The darkness stands for the way that the Christless life is filled with things which seek the shadows because they cannot stand the light.

(vi) The darkness is characteristically unfruitful. Paul speaks of the unfruitful works of darkness (*Ephesians* 5: 11). If growing things are despoiled of the light, their growth is arrested. The darkness is the Christless atmosphere in which no fruit of the Spirit will ever grow.

(vii) The darkness is connected with lovelessness and hate. If a man hates his brother, it is a sign that he walks in darkness (1 *John* 2: 9–11). Love is sunshine and hatred is the dark.

(viii) The dark is the abode of the enemies of Christ and the final goal of those who will not accept him. The struggle of the Christian and of Christ is against the hostile rulers of the darkness of this world (*Ephesians* 6: 12). Consistent and rebellious sinners are those for whom the mist of darkness is reserved (2 *Peter* 2: 9; *Jude* 13). The darkness is the life which is separated from God.

THE NECESSITY OF WALKING IN THE LIGHT

1 *John* 1: 6, 7

> If we say that we have fellowship with him and at the same time walk in darkness, we lie and are not doing the truth. But if we walk in the light, as he is in the light, we have fellowship with each other and the blood of Jesus Christ is steadily cleansing us from all sin.

HERE John is writing to counteract one heretical way of thought. There were those who claimed to be specially intellectually and spiritually advanced, but whose lives showed no sign of it. They claimed to have advanced so far along the road of knowledge and of spirituality that for them sin had ceased to matter and the laws had ceased to exist. Napoleon once said that laws were made for ordinary people, but were never meant for the like of him. So these heretics claimed to be so far on that, even if they did sin, it was of no importance whatsoever. In later days Clement of

Alexandria tells us that there were heretics who said that it
made no difference how a man lived. Irenaeus tells us that
they declared that a truly spiritual man was quite incapable
of ever incurring any pollution, no matter what kind of deeds
he did.

In answer John insists on certain things.

(i) He insists that to have fellowship with the God who
is light a man must walk in the light and that, if he is still
walking in the moral and ethical darkness of the Christless
life, he can not have that fellowship. This is precisely what
the Old Testament had said centuries before. God said, "You
shall be holy; for I the Lord your God am Holy" (*Leviticus*
19: 2; cp. 20: 7, 26). He who would find fellowship with God
is committed to a life of goodness which reflects God's
goodness. C. H. Dodd writes: "The Church is a society of
people who, believing in a God of pure goodness, accept the
obligation to be good like him." This does not mean that a
man must be perfect before he can have fellowship with God;
if that were the case, all of us would be shut out. But it
does mean that he will spend his whole life in the awareness
of his obligations, in the effort to fulfil them and in penitence
when he fails. It will mean that he will never think that
sin does not matter; it will mean that the nearer he comes
to God, the more terrible sin will be to him.

(ii) He insists that these mistaken thinkers have the wrong
idea of truth. He says that, if people who claim to be specially
advanced still walk in darkness, they are not *doing* the truth.
Exactly the same phrase is used in the Fourth Gospel, when
it speaks of him, who does the truth (*John* 3: 21). This means
that for the Christian truth is never only intellectual; it is
always moral. It is not something which exercises only the
mind; it is something which exercises the whole personality.
Truth is not only the discovery of abstract things; it is con-
crete living. It is not only thinking; it is also acting. The
words which the New Testament uses along with *truth* are
significant. It speaks of *obeying* the truth (*Romans* 2: 8;
Galatians 3: 7); *following* the truth (*Galatians* 2: 14; 3 *John* 4);

of *opposing* the truth (2 *Timothy* 3: 8); of *wandering from* the truth (*James* 5: 19). There is such a thing as might be called "discussion circle Christianity." It is possible to look on Christianity as a series of intellectual problems to be solved and on the Bible as a book about which illuminating information is to be amassed. But Christianity is something to be followed and the Bible a book to be obeyed. It is possible for intellectual eminence and moral failure to go hand in hand. For the Christian the truth is something first to be discovered and then to be obeyed.

THE TESTS OF TRUTH

1 *John* 1: 6, 7 (*continued*)

As John sees it, there are two great tests of truth.

(i) Truth is the creator of fellowship. If men are really walking in the light, they have fellowship one with another. No belief can be fully Christian if it separates a man from his fellow-men. No Church can be exclusive and still be the Church of Christ. That which destroys fellowship cannot be true.

(ii) He who really knows the truth is daily more and more cleansed from sin by the blood of Jesus. The Revised Standard Version is correct enough here but it can very easily be misunderstood. It runs: "The blood of Jesus his Son cleanses us from all sin." That can be read as a statement of a general principle. But it is a statement of what ought to be happening in the individual life. The meaning is that all the time, day by day, constantly and consistently, the blood of Jesus Christ ought to be carrying out a cleansing process in the life of the individual Christian.

The Greek for *to cleanse* is *katharizein* which was originally a ritual word, describing the ceremonies and washings and so on which qualified a man to approach his gods. But the word, as religion developed, came to have a moral sense; and it describes the goodness which enables a man to enter into the presence of God. So what John is saying is, "If you really know what the sacrifice of Christ has done and are really experiencing its power, day by day you will be adding holiness to your life and becoming more fit to enter the presence of God."

Here indeed is a great conception. It looks on the sacrifice of Christ as something which not only atones for past sin but equips a man in holiness day by day.

True religion is that by which every day a man comes closer to his fellow-men and closer to God. It produces fellowship with God and fellowship with men—and we can never have the one without the other.

THE THREEFOLD LIE

1 *John* 1: 6, 7 (*continued*)

FOUR times in his letter John bluntly accuses the false teachers of being liars; and the first of these occasions is in this present passage.

(i) Those who claim to have fellowship with the God who is altogether light and who yet walk in the dark are lying (verse 6). A little later he repeats this charge in a slightly different way. The man who says that he knows God and yet does not keep God's commandments is a liar (1 *John* 2: 4). John is laying down the blunt truth that the man who says one thing with his lips and another thing with his life is a liar. He is not thinking of the man who tries his hardest and yet often fails. "A man," said H. G. Wells, "may be a very bad musician, and may yet be passionately in love with music"; and a man may be very conscious of his failures and yet be passionately in love with Christ and the way of Christ. John is thinking of the man who makes the highest possible claims to knowledge, to intellectual eminence and to spirituality, and who yet allows himself things which he well knows are forbidden. The man who professes to love Christ and deliberately disobeys him, is guilty of a lie.

(ii) The man who denies that Jesus is the Christ is a liar (1 *John* 2: 22). Here is something which runs through the whole New Testament. The ultimate test of any man is his reaction to Jesus. The ultimate question which Jesus asks every man is: "Who do you say that I am?" (*Matthew* 16: 13). A man confronted with Christ cannot but see the greatness that is there; and, if he denies it, he is a liar.

(iii) The man who says that he loves God and at the same time hates his brother is a liar (1 *John* 4: 20). Love of God and hatred of man cannot exist in the same person. If there is bitterness in a man's heart towards any other, that is proof that he does not really love God. All our protestations of love to God are useless if there is hatred in our hearts towards any man.

THE SINNER'S SELF-DECEPTION

1 *John* 1: 8–10

> If we say that we have no sin, we deceive ourselves and the truth is not in us. If we confess our sins, we can rely on him in his righteousness to forgive us our sins and to make us clean from all unrighteousness.
>
> If we say that we have not sinned, we make him a liar and his word is not in us.

IN this passage John describes and condemns two further mistaken ways of thought.

(i) There is the man who says that he has no sin. That may mean either of two things.

It may describe the man who says that he has no responsibility for his sin. It is easy enough to find defences behind which to seek to hide. We may blame our sins on our heredity, on our environment, on our temperament, on our physical condition. We may claim that someone misled us and that we were led astray. It is characteristic of us all that we seek to shuffle out of the responsibility for sin. Or it may describe the man who claims that he can sin and take no harm.

It is John's insistence that, when a man has sinned, excuses and self-justifications are irrelevant. The only thing which will meet the situation is humble and penitent confession to God and, if need be, to men.

Then John says a surprising thing. He says that we can depend on God *in his righteousness* to forgive us if we confess our sins. On the face of it, we might well have thought that God *in his righteousness* would have been much more likely to condemn than to forgive. But the point is that God, because he is righteous, never breaks his word; and Scripture is full of the promise of mercy to the man who comes to him with penitent heart. God has promised that he will never despise the contrite heart and he will not break his word. If we humbly and sorrowfully confess our sins, he will forgive. The very fact of making excuses and seeking for self-justification debars us from forgiveness, because it debars us from penitence; the very fact of humble confession opens the door to forgiveness, for the man with the penitent heart can claim the promises of God.

(ii) There is the man who says that he has not in fact sinned. That attitude is not nearly so uncommon as we might think. Any number of people do not really believe that they have sinned and rather resent being called sinners. Their mistake is that they think of sin as the kind of thing which gets into the newspapers. They forget that sin is *hamartia* which literally means a *missing of the target*. To fail to be as good a father, mother, wife, husband, son, daughter, workman, person as we might be is to sin; and that includes us all.

In any event the man who says that he has not sinned is in effect doing nothing less than calling God a liar, for God has said that all have sinned.

So John condemns the man who claims that he is so far advanced in knowledge and in the spiritual life that sin for him has ceased to matter; he condemns the man who evades the responsibility for his sin or who holds that sin has no effect upon him; he condemns the man who has never even realized that he is a sinner. The essence of the Christian life is first to realize our sin; and then to go to God for that forgiveness which can wipe out the past and for that cleansing which can make the future new.

A PASTOR'S CONCERN

1 *John* 2: 1, 2

> My little children, I am writing these things to you that you may not sin. But, if anyone does sin, we have one who will plead our cause to the Father, Jesus Christ the righteous. For he is the propitiating sacrifice for our sins, and not for ours only but also for the whole world.

THE first thing to note in this passage is the sheer affection in it. John begins with the address, "My little children." Both in Latin and in Greek diminutives carry a special affection. They are words which are used, as it were, with a caress. John is a very old man; he must be, in fact, the last survivor of his generation, maybe the last man alive who had walked and talked with Jesus in the days of his flesh. So often age gets out of sympathy with youth and acquires even an impatient irritableness with the new and laxer ways of the younger generation. But not John; in his old age he has nothing but tenderness for those who are his little children in the faith. He is writing to tell them that they must not sin but he does not scold. There is no cutting edge in his voice; he seeks to love them into goodness. In this opening address there is the yearning, affectionate tenderness of a pastor for people whom he has known for long in all their wayward foolishness and still loves.

His object in writing is that they may not sin. There is a two-fold connection of thought here—with what has gone before and with what comes afterwards. There is a two-fold danger that they may indeed think lightly of sin.

John says two things about sin. First, he has just said that sin is universal; anyone who says that he has not sinned is a liar. Second, there is forgiveness of sins through what Jesus Christ has done, and still does, for men. Now it would be possible to use both these statements as an excuse to think lightly of sin. If all have sinned, why make a fuss about it and what is the use of struggling against something which is in any event an inevitable part of the human situation? Again, if there is forgiveness of sins, why worry about it?

In face of that, John, as Westcott points out, has two things to say.

First, the Christian is one who has come to know God; and the inevitable accompaniment of knowledge must be *obedience*. We shall return to this more fully; but at the moment we note that to know God and to obey God must, as John sees it, be twin parts of the same experience.

Second, the man who claims that he abides in God (verse 6) and in Jesus Christ must live the same kind of life as Jesus lived. That is to say, union with Christ necessarily involves *imitation* of Christ.

So John lays down his two great ethical principles; knowledge involves obedience, and union involves imitation. Therefore, in the Christian life there can never be any inducement to think lightly of sin.

JESUS CHRIST THE PARACLETE

1 *John* 2: 1, 2 (*continued*)

IT will take us some considerable time to deal with these two verses for there are hardly any other two in the New Testament which so succinctly set out the work of Christ.

Let us first set out the problem. It is clear that Christianity is an ethical religion; that is what John is concerned to stress. But it is also clear that man is so often an ethical failure. Confronted with the demands of God, he

admits them and accepts them—and then fails to keep them.
Here, then, there is a barrier erected between man and God.
How can man, the sinner, ever enter into the presence of
God, the all-holy? That problem is solved in Jesus Christ.
And in this passage John uses two great words about Jesus
Christ which we must study, not simply to acquire intellectual
knowledge but to understand and so to enter into the benefits
of Christ.

He calls Jesus Christ our *Advocate with the Father*. The
word is *paraklētos* which in the Fourth Gospel the Authorized
Version translates *Comforter*. It is so great a word and has
behind it so great a thought that we must examine it in
detail. *Paraklētos* comes from the verb *parakalein*. There are
occasions when *parakalein* means *to comfort*. It is, for instance,
used with that meaning in *Genesis* 37:35, where it is said
that all Jacob's sons and daughters rose up to *comfort* him at
the loss of Joseph; in *Isaiah* 61:2, where it is said that the
function of the prophet is to *comfort* all that mourn; and
in *Matthew* 5:4, where it is said that those who mourn will
be *comforted*.

But that is neither the commonest nor the most literal sense
of *parakalein*; its commonest sense is *to call someone to one's
side* in order to use him in some way as a helper and a
counsellor. In ordinary Greek that is a very common usage.
Xenophon (*Anabasis* 1.6.5) tells how Cyrus *summoned* (*parakalein*) Clearchos into his tent to be his counsellor, for
Clearchos was a man held in the highest honour by Cyrus
and by the Greeks. Aeschines, the Greek orator, protests
against his opponents calling in Demosthenes, his great rival,
and says: "Why need you *call* Demosthenes *to your support*?
To do so is *to call in* a rascally rhetorician to cheat the ears
of the jury" (*Against Ctesiphon* 200).

Paraklētos itself is a word which is passive in form and
literally means *someone who is called to one's side*; but since it
is always the reason for the calling in that is uppermost in
the mind, the word, although passive in form, has an active
sense, and comes to mean a helper, a supporter and, above

all, a witness in someone's favour, an advocate in someone's defence. It too is a common word in ordinary secular Greek. Demosthenes (*De Fals. Leg.* 1) speaks of the importunities and the party spirit of *advocates* (*paraklētoi*) serving the ends of private ambition instead of public good. Diogenes Laertius (4: 50) tells of a caustic saying of the philosopher Bion. A very talkative person sought his help in some matter. Bion said, "I will do what you want, if you will only send someone to me to plead your case (i.e., send a *paraklētos*), and stay away yourself." When Philo is telling the story of Joseph and his brethren, he says that, when Joseph forgave them for the wrong that they had done him, he said, "I offer you an amnesty for all that you did to me; you need no other *paraklētos*" (*Life of Joseph* 40). Philo tells how the Jews of Alexandria were being oppressed by a certain governor and determined to take their case to the emperor. "We must find," they said, "a more powerful *paraklētos* by whom the Emperor Gaius will be brought to a favourable disposition towards us" (*Leg. in Flacc.* 968 B).

So common was this word that it came into other languages just as it stood. In the New Testament itself the Syriac, Egyptian, Arabic, and Ethiopic versions all keep the word *paraklētos* just as it stands. The Jews especially adopted the word and used it in this sense of *advocate*, someone to plead one's cause. They used it as the opposite of the word *accuser* and the Rabbis had this saying about what would happen in the day of God's judgment. "The man who keeps one commandment of the Law has gotten to himself one *paraklētos*; the man who breaks one commandment of the Law has gotten to himself one accuser." They said, "If a man is summoned to court on a capital charge, he needs powerful *paraklētoi* (the plural of the word) to save him; repentance and good works are his *paraklētoi* in the judgment of God." "All the righteousness and mercy which an Israelite does in this world are great peace and great *paraklētoi* between him and his father in heaven." They said that the sin-offering is a man's *paraklētos* before God.

So the word came into the Christian vocabulary. In the days of the persecutions and the martyrs, a Christian pleader called Vettius Epagathos ably pled the case of those who were accused of being Christians. "He was an advocate (*paraklētos*) for the Christians, for he had the Advocate within himself, even the Spirit" (Eusebius: *The Ecclesiastical History* 5: 1). The Letter of Barnabas (20) speaks of evil men who are the *advocates* of the wealthy and the unjust judges of the poor. The writer of Second Clement asks: "Who shall be your *paraklētos* if it be not clear that your works are righteous and holy?" (2 *Clement* 6: 9).

A *paraklētos* has been defined as "one who lends his presence to his friends." More than once in the New Testament there is this great conception of Jesus as the friend and the defender of man. In a military court-martial the officer who defends the soldier under accusation is called the prisoner's friend. Jesus is our friend. Paul writes of that Christ who is at the right hand of God and "who intercedes for us" (*Romans* 8: 34). The writer of the Letter to the Hebrews speaks of Jesus Christ as the one who "ever lives to make intercession" for men (*Hebrews* 7: 25); and he also speaks of him as "appearing in the presence of God for us" (*Hebrews* 9: 24).

The tremendous thing about Jesus is that he has never lost his interest in, or his love for, men. We are not to think of him as having gone through his life upon the earth and his death upon the Cross, and then being finished with men. He still bears his concern for us upon his heart; he still pleads for us; Jesus Christ is the prisoner's friend for all.

JESUS CHRIST THE PROPITIATION

1 *John* 2: 1, 2 (*continued*)

JOHN goes on to say that Jesus is *the propitiation for our sins*. The word is *hilasmos*. This is a more difficult picture for us fully to grasp. The picture of the *advocate* is universal for all men have experience of a friend coming to their aid; but the picture in *propitiation* is from *sacrifice* and is more natural to the Jewish mind than to ours. To understand it we must get at the basic ideas behind it.

The great aim of all religion is fellowship with God, to know him as friend and to enter with joy, and not fear, into his presence. It therefore follows that the supreme problem of religion is sin, for it is sin that interrupts fellowship with God. It is to meet that problem that all sacrifice arises. By sacrifice fellowship with God is restored. So the Jews offered, night and morning, the sin-offering in the Temple. That was the offering, not for any particular sin but for man as a sinner; and so long as the Temple lasted it was made to God in the morning and in the evening. The Jews also offered their trespass-offerings to God; these were the offerings for particular sins. The Jews had their Day of Atonement, whose ritual was designed to atone for *all* sins, known and unknown. It is with that background that we must come at this picture of propitiation.

As we have said, the Greek word for *propitiation* is *hilasmos*, and the corresponding verb is *hilaskesthai*. This verb has three meanings. (i) When it is used with a man as the subject, it means *to placate* or *to pacify* someone who has been injured or offended, and especially to placate a god. It is to bring a sacrifice or to perform a ritual whereby a god, offended by sin, is placated. (ii) If the subject is *God*, the verb means *to forgive*, for then the meaning is that God himself provides the means whereby the lost relationship between him and men is restored. (iii) The third meaning is allied with the first. The verb often means to perform some deed, by which the taint of guilt is removed. A man sins; at once he acquires the taint of sin; he needs something, which, to use C. H. Dodd's metaphor, will *disinfect* him from that taint and enable him once again to enter into the presence of God. In that sense *hilaskesthai* means, not to propitiate but to *expiate*, not so much to pacify God as to disinfect man from the taint of sin and thereby fit him again to enter into fellowship with God.

When John says that Jesus is the *hilasmos* for our sins, he is, we think, bringing all these different senses into one. Jesus is the person through whom guilt for past sin and defilement from present sin are removed. The great basic truth behind this word is that it is through Jesus Christ that man's fellowship with God is first restored and then maintained.

We note one other thing. As John sees it, this work of Jesus was carried out not only for us but for the whole world. There is in the New Testament a strong line of thought in which the universality of the salvation of God is stressed. God so loved *the world* that he sent his son (*John* 3: 16). Jesus is confident that, if he is lifted up, he will draw *all men* to him (*John* 12: 32). God will have *all men* to be saved (1 *Timothy* 2: 4). He would be a bold man who would set limits to the grace and love of God or to the effectiveness of the work and sacrifice of Jesus Christ. Truly the love of God is broader than the measures of man's mind; and in the New Testament itself there are hints of a salvation whose arms are as wide as the world.

THE TRUE KNOWLEDGE OF GOD

1 *John* 2: 3–6

And it is by this that we know that we have come to know him—if we keep his commandments. He who says, "I have come to know him" and who does not keep his commandments is a liar, and the truth is not in such a man. The love of God is truly perfected in any man who keeps his word. This is the way in which we know that we are in him. He who claims that he abides in him ought himself to live the same kind of life as he lived.

THIS passage deals in phrases and thoughts which were very

familiar to the ancient world. It talked much about *knowing God* and about *being in God*. It is important that we should see wherein the difference lay between the pagan world in all its greatness and Judaism and Christianity. To know God, to abide in God, to have fellowship with God has always been the quest of the human spirit, for Augustine was right when he said that God had made men for himself and that they were restless until they found their rest in him. We may say that in the ancient world there were three lines of thought in regard to knowing God.

(i) In the great classical age of their thought and literature, in the sixth and fifth centuries before Christ, the Greeks were convinced that they could arrive at God by the sheer process of intellectual reasoning and argument. In *The World of the New Testament*, T. R. Glover has a chapter on *The Greek* in which he brilliantly and vividly sketches the character of the Greek mind in its greatest days when the Greek glorified the intellect. "A harder and more precise thinker than Plato it will be difficult to discover," said Marshall Macgregor. Xenophon tells how Socrates had a conversation with a young man. "How do you know that?" asked Socrates. "Do you know it or are you guessing?" The young man had to say, "I am guessing." "Very well," answered Socrates, "when we are done with guessing and when we know, shall we talk about it then?" Guesses were not good enough for the Greek thinker.

To the classical Greek curiosity was not a fault but was the greatest of the virtues, for it was the mother of philosophy. Glover writes of this outlook: "Everything must be examined; all the world is the proper study of man; there is no question which it is wrong for man to ask; nature in the long run must stand and deliver; God too must explain himself, for did he not make man so?" For the Greeks of the great classical age the way to God was by the intellect.

It has to be noted that an intellectual approach to religion is not necessarily ethical at all. If religion is a series of mental problems, if God is the goal at the end of intense mental activity, religion becomes something not very unlike the higher mathematics. It becomes intellectual satisfaction and not moral action; and the plain fact is that many of the great Greek thinkers were not specially good men. Even men so great as Plato and Socrates saw no sin in homosexuality. A man could know God in the intellectual sense but that need not make him a good man.

(ii) The later Greeks, in the immediate background time of the New Testament, sought to find God in emotional experience. The characteristic religious phenomenon of these days was the Mystery Religions. In any view of the history of religion they are an amazing feature. Their aim was union with the divine and they were all in the form of passion plays. They were all founded on the story of some god who lived, and suffered terribly, and died a cruel death, and rose again. The initiate was given a long course of instruction; he was made to practise ascetic discipline. He was worked up to an intense pitch of expectation and emotional sensitivity. He was then allowed to come to a passion play in which the story of the suffering, dying, and rising god was played out on the stage. Everything was designed to heighten the emotional atmosphere. There was cunning lighting; sensuous music; perfumed incense; a marvellous liturgy. In this atmosphere the story was played out and the worshipper identified himself with the experiences of the god until he could cry out: "I am thou, and thou art I"; until he shared the god's suffering and also shared his victory and immortality.

This was not so much *knowing* God as *feeling* God. But it was a highly emotional experience and, as such, it was necessarily transient. It was a kind of religious drug. It quite definitely found God in an abnormal experience and its aim was to escape from ordinary life.

(iii) Lastly, there was the Jewish way of knowing God which is closely allied with the Christian way. To the Jew knowledge of God came, not by man's speculation or by an exotic experience of emotion, but by God's own revelation. The God who revealed himself was a holy God and his holiness brought the obligation to his worshipper to be holy, too. A. E. Brooke says, "John can conceive of no real knowledge of God which does not issue in obedience." Knowledge of God can be proved only by obedience to God; and knowledge of God can be gained only by obedience to God. C. H. Dodd says, "To know God is to experience his love in Christ, and to return that love in obedience."

Here was John's problem. In the Greek world he was faced with people who saw God as an intellectual exercise and who could say, "I know God" without being conscious of any ethical obligation whatever. In the Greek world he was faced with people who had had an emotional experience and who could say, "I am in God and God is in me," and who yet did not see God in terms of commandments at all.

John is determined to lay it down quite unmistakably and without compromise that the only way in which we can show that we know God is by obedience to him, and the only way we can show that we have union with Christ is by imitation of him. Christianity is the religion which offers the greatest privilege and brings with it the greatest obligation. Intellectual effort and emotional experience are not neglected—far from it—but they must combine to issue in moral action.

THE COMMANDMENT WHICH IS OLD AND NEW

1 *John* 2: 7, 8

> Beloved, it is not a new commandment which I am writing to you, but an old commandment which you had from the beginning; the old commandment is the word which you heard. Again, it is a new commandment which I am writing to you, a thing which is true in him and in you, because the darkness is passing away and the light is now shining.

Beloved is John's favourite address to his people (cp. 3: 2,

21; 4: 1, 7; 3 *John* 1, 2, 5, 11). The whole accent of his writing is love. As Westcott puts it: "St. John, while enforcing the commandment of love, gives expression to it." There is something very lovely here. So much of this letter is a warning; and parts of it are rebuke. When we are warning people or rebuking them, it is so easy to become coldly critical; it is so easy to scold; it is even possible to take a cruel pleasure in seeing people wince under our verbal lash. But, even when he has to say hard things, the accent of John's voice is love. He had learned the lesson which every parent, every preacher, every teacher, every leader must learn; he had learned to speak the truth in love.

John speaks about a commandment which is at one and the same time old and new. Some would take this as referring to the implied commandment in verse 6 that he who abides in Jesus Christ must live the same kind of life as his Master lived. But almost certainly John is thinking of the words of Jesus in the Fourth Gospel: "A new commandment I give to you, That you love one another; even as I have loved you, that you also love one another" (*John* 13: 34). In what sense was that commandment both old and new?

(i) It was old in the sense that it was already there in the Old Testament. Did not the Law say, "Thou shalt love thy neighbour as thyself"? (*Leviticus* 19: 18). It was old in the sense that this was not the first time that John's hearers had heard it. From the very first day of their entry into the Christian life they had been taught that the law of love must be the law of their lives. This commandment went a long way back in history and a long way back in the lives of those to whom John was speaking.

(ii) It was new in that it had been raised to a completely new standard in the life of Jesus—and it was as Jesus had loved men that men were now to love each other. It could well be said that men did not really know what love was until they saw it in him. In every sphere of life it is possible for a thing to be old in the sense that it has for long existed and yet to reach a completely new standard in

someone's performance of it. A game may become a new
game to a man when he has seen some master play it. A
piece of music may become a new thing to a man when
he has heard some great orchestra play it under the baton
of some master conductor. Even a dish of food can become a
new thing to a man when he tastes it after it has been
prepared by someone with a genius for cooking. An old
thing can become a new experience in the hands of a master.
In Jesus love became new in two directions.

(*a*) It became new in *the extent to which it reached*. In
Jesus love reached out *to the sinner*. To the orthodox Jewish
Rabbi the sinner was a person whom God wished to destroy.
"There is joy in heaven," they said, "when one sinner is
obliterated from the earth." But Jesus was the friend of out-
cast men and women and of sinners, and he was sure that
there was joy in heaven when one sinner came home. In
Jesus love reached out *to the Gentile*. As the Rabbis saw it:
"The Gentiles were created by God to be fuel for the fires
of Hell." But in Jesus God so loved *the world* that he gave
his Son. Love became new in Jesus because he widened its
boundaries until there were none outside its embrace.

(*b*) It became new in *the lengths to which it would go*. No
lack of response, nothing that men could ever do to him,
could turn Jesus's love to hate. He could even pray for God's
mercy on those who were nailing him to his Cross.

The commandment to love was old in the sense that men
had known of it for long; but it was new because in Jesus
Christ love had reached a standard which it had never reached
before and it was by that standard that men were bidden
to love.

THE DEFEAT OF THE DARK

1 *John* 2: 7, 8 (*continued*)

JOHN goes on to say that this commandment of love is true
in Jesus Christ and true in the people to whom he is writing.

To John, as we have seen, truth was not only something to be grasped with the mind; it was something to be done. What he means is that the commandment to love one another is the highest truth; in Jesus Christ we can see that commandment in all the glory of its fullness; in him that commandment is true; and in the Christian we can see it, not in the fullness of its truth but coming true. For John, Christianity is progress in love.

He goes on to say that the light is shining and the darkness is passing away. This must be read in context. By the time John wrote, at the end of the first century, men's ideas were changing. In the very early days they had looked for the Second Coming of Jesus as a sudden and shattering event within their own life time. When that did not happen, they did not abandon the hope but allowed experience to change it. To John the Second Coming of Christ is not one sudden, dramatic event but a process in which the darkness is steadily being defeated by the light; and the end of the process will be a world in which the darkness is totally defeated and the light triumphant.

In this passage and in verses 10 and 11, the light is identified with love and the dark with hate. That is to say, the end of this process is a world where love reigns supreme and hate is banished for ever. Christ has come in the individual heart when a man's whole being is ruled by love; and he will have come in the world of men when all men obey his commandment of love. The coming and reign of Jesus is identical with the coming and reign of love.

LOVE AND HATE, AND LIGHT AND DARK

1 *John* 2: 9–11

He who says that he is in the light, and who at the same time hates his brother, is still in the darkness. He who loves his brother abides in the light, and there is nothing in him which makes him stumble. He who hates his brother is in the darkness and he is walking in darkness, and he does not know where he is going, because the darkness has blinded his eyes.

THE first thing which strikes us about this passage is the way in which John sees personal relationships in terms of black and white. In regard to our brother man, it is a case of either love or hate; as John sees it, there is no such thing as neutrality in personal relationships. As Westcott put it: "Indifference is impossible; there is no twilight in the spiritual world."

It is further to be noted that what John is speaking about is a man's attitude to his *brother*, that is, to the man next door, the man beside whom he lives and works, the man with whom he comes into contact every day. There is a kind of Christian attitude which enthusiastically preaches love to people in other lands, but has never sought any kind of fellowship with its next door neighbour or even managed to live at peace within its own family circle. John insists on love for the man with whom we are in daily contact. As A. E. Brooke puts it, this is not "vapid philosophy, or a pretentious cosmopolitanism"; it is immediate and practical.

John was perfectly right when he drew his sharp distinction between light and dark, love and hate, without shades and halfway stages. Our brother cannot be disregarded; he is part of the landscape. The question is *how* do we regard him?

(i) We may regard our brother man as *negligible*. We can make all our plans without taking him into our calculations at all. We can live on the assumption that his need and his sorrow and his welfare and his salvation have nothing to do with us. A man may be so self-centred—often quite unconsciously—that in his world no one matters except himself.

(ii) We may regard our brother man with *contempt*. We may treat him as a fool in comparison with our intellectual attainment and as one whose opinions are to be brushed aside. We may regard him much as the Greeks regarded slaves, a necessary lesser breed, useful enough for the menial duties of life, but not to be compared with themselves.

(iii) We may regard our brother man as a *nuisance*. We may feel that law and convention have given him a certain claim upon us, but that claim is nothing more than an unfortunate necessity. Thus a man may regard any gift he has to make to charity and any tax he has to pay for social welfare as regrettable. Some in their heart of hearts regard those who are in poverty or in sickness and those who are under-privileged as mere nuisances.

(iv) We may regard our brother man as an *enemy*. If we regard competition as the principle of life, that is bound to be so. Every other man in the same profession or trade is a potential competitor and, therefore, a potential enemy.

(v) We may regard our brother man as a *brother*. We may regard his needs as our needs, his interests as our interests, and to be in fellowship with him as the true joy of life.

THE EFFECT OF LOVE AND HATE

1 *John* 2: 9–11 (*continued*)

JOHN has something further to say. As he sees it, our attitude to our brother man has an effect not only on him but also on ourselves.

(i) If we love our brother, we are walking in the light and there is nothing in us which causes us to stumble. The Greek could mean that, if we love our brother, there is nothing in us which causes *others* to stumble and, of course, that would be perfectly true. But it is much more likely that John is saying that, if we love our brother, there is nothing in us which causes *ourselves* to stumble. That is to say, love enables us to make progress in the spiritual life and hatred makes progress impossible. When we think of it, that is perfectly obvious. If God is love and if the new commandment of Christ is love, then love brings us nearer to men and to God and hatred separates us from men and from God.

We ought always to remember that he who has in his heart
hatred, resentment and the unforgiving spirit, can never grow
up in the spiritual life.

(ii) John goes on to say that he who hates his brother
walks in darkness and does not know where he is going,
because the darkness has blinded him. That is to say, hatred
makes a man blind and this, too, is perfectly obvious. When
a man has hatred in his heart, his powers of judgment are
obscured; he cannot see an issue clearly. It is no uncommon
sight to see a man opposing a good proposal simply because
he dislikes, or has quarrelled with, the man who made it.
Again and again progress in some scheme of a church or
an association is held up because of personal animosities.
No man is fit to give a verdict on anything while he has
hatred in his heart; and no man can rightly direct his own
life when hatred dominates him.

Love enables a man to walk in the light; hatred leaves
him in the dark—even if he does not realise that it is so.

REMEMBERING WHO WE ARE

1 *John* 2: 12-14

I am writing to you, little children,
  Because your sins are forgiven you through his name.
I am writing to you, fathers,
  Because you have come to know him who is from
  the beginning.
I am writing to you, young men,
  Because you have overcome the Evil One.
I have written to you, little ones,
  Because you have come to know the Father.
I have written to you, fathers,
  Because you have come to know him who is from
  the beginning.
I have written to you, young men,
  Because you are strong,
  And the word of God abides in you,
  And you have overcome the Evil One.

THIS is a very lovely passage and yet for all its beauty it
has its problems of interpretation. We may begin by noting
two things which are certain.

First, as to its form, this passage is not exactly poetry
but it is certainly poetical and strongly rhythmical. Therefore,
it is to be interpreted as poetry ought to be.

Second, as to its contents, John has been warning his people
of the perils of the dark and the necessity of walking in the
light and now he says that in every case their best defence
is to remember what they are and what has been done for
them. No matter who they are, their sins have been forgiven;
no matter who they are, they know him who is from the
beginning; no matter who they are, they have the strength
which can face and overcome the Evil One. When Nehemiah
was urged to seek a cowardly safety, his answer was:
"Should such a man as I flee?" (*Nehemiah* 6: 11). And when
the Christian is tempted, his answer may well be: "Should
such a man as I stoop to this folly or stain my hands
with this evil?" The man who is forgiven, who knows God
and who is aware that he can draw on a strength beyond
his own, has a great defence against temptation in simply
remembering these things.

But in this passage there are problems. The first is quite
simple. Why does John say three times *I am writing* and three
times *I have written*? The Vulgate translates both by the
present tense *scribo*; and it has been argued that John varies
the tense simply to avoid the monotony that six successive
present tenses would bring. It has also been argued that the
past tenses are what Greek calls the *epistolary aorist*. Greek
letter-writers had a habit of using the past instead of the
present tense because they put themselves in the position of
the reader. To the *writer* of a letter a thing may be *present*
because at the moment he is doing it; but to the *reader* of
the letter it will be *past* because by that time it has been
done. To take a simple instance, a Greek letter-writer might
equally well say, "I am going to town today," or "I went
to town today." That is the Greek *epistolary* or *letter-writer's*

aorist. If that be the case here, there is no real difference between John's *I am writing* and *I have written*.

More likely the explanation is this. When John says *I am writing* he is thinking of what he is at the moment writing and of what he still has to say; when he says *I have written* he is thinking of what has already been written and his readers have already read. The sense would then be that the whole letter, the part already written, the part being written and the part still to come, is all designed to remind Christians of who and whose they are and of what has been done for them.

For John it was of supreme importance that the Christian should remember the status and the benefits he has in Jesus Christ, for these would be his defence against error and against sin.

AT EVERY STAGE

1 *John* 2: 12-14 (*continued*)

THE second problem which confronts us is more difficult, and also more important. John uses three titles of the people to whom he is writing. He calls them *little children*; in verse 12 the Greek is *teknia* and in verse 13 *paidia*; *teknia* indicates a child young in age and *paidia* a child young in experience, and, therefore, in need of training and discipline. He calls them *fathers*. He calls them *young men*. The question then is: to whom is John writing and three answers have been given.

(i) It is suggested that we are to take these words as representing three age groups in the church—children, fathers, and young men. The *children* have the sweet innocence of childhood and of forgiveness. The *fathers* have the mature wisdom which Christian experience can bring. The *young* men have the strength which enables them to win their personal battle with the Evil One. That is most attractive; but there are three reasons which make us hesitate to adopt it as the only meaning of the passage.

(*a*) *Little children* is one of John's favourite expressions.
He also uses it in 2: 1, 28; 3: 7; 4: 4; 5: 21; and it is clear in
the other cases that he is not thinking of *little children* in
terms of age but of Christians whose spiritual father he is.
By this time he must have been very nearly a hundred years
old; all the members of his churches were of a far younger
generation and to him they were all little children in the same
way as a teacher or professor may still think of his *boys*
after the boys have long since become men.

(*b*) The fact that the passage is kin to poetry makes us
think twice before insisting that so literal a meaning must
be given to the words and so cut and dried a classification
be taken as intended. Literalism and poetry do not go com-
fortably hand in hand.

(*c*) Perhaps the greatest difficulty is that the blessings of
which John speaks are not the exclusive possession of any
one age group. Forgiveness does not belong to the child
alone; a Christian may be young in the faith, and yet have a
wonderful maturity; strength to overcome the tempter does
not—thank God—belong to youth alone. These blessings are
the blessings not of any one age but of the Christian life.

We do not say that there is no thought of age groups in
this. There almost certainly is; but John has a way of saying
things which can be taken in two ways, a narrower and a
wider; and, while the narrower meaning is here, we must go
beyond it to find the full meaning.

(ii) It is suggested that we are to find two groups here.
The argument is that *little children* describes *Christians in
general* and that Christians in general are then divided into
two groups, the fathers and the young men, that is, the young
and the old, the mature and the as yet immature. That is
perfectly possible, because John's people must have become
so used to hearing him call them *my little children* that they
would not connect the words with age at all but would
always include themselves in that address.

(iii) It is suggested that in every case the words include
all Christians and that no classification is intended. *All*

Christians are like little children, for all can regain their innocence by the forgiveness of Jesus Christ. *All* Christians are like fathers, like full-grown, responsible men, who can think and learn their way deeper and deeper into the knowledge of Jesus Christ. *All* Christians are like young men, with a vigorous strength to fight and win their battles against the tempter and his power. It seems to us that indeed this is John's wider meaning. We may begin by taking his words as a classification of Christians into three age groups; but we come to see that the blessings of each group are the blessings of all the groups and that each one of us finds himself included in all of them.

GOD'S GIFTS IN CHRIST

1 *John* 2: 12–14 (*continued*)

THIS passage finely sets out God's gifts to all men in Jesus Christ.

(i) There is the gift of *forgiveness through Jesus Christ*. This was the essential message of the gospel and of the early preachers. They were sent out to preach repentance and remission of sins (*Luke* 24: 47). It was Paul's message at Antioch in Pisidia that to men there was proclaimed through Jesus Christ forgiveness of sins (*Acts* 13: 38). To be forgiven is to be at peace with God—and that is precisely the gift that Jesus brought to men.

John uses the curious phrase *through his name* (verse 12). Forgiveness comes *through the name* of Jesus Christ. The Jews used *the name* in a very special way. The name is not simply that by which a person is called; it stands for the whole character of a person in so far as it has been made known to men. This use is very common in the Book of Psalms. "Those who know thy name put their trust in thee" (*Psalm* 9: 10). This clearly does not mean that those who know that God is called *Jahweh* will put their trust in him;

it means that those who know God's nature in so far as it has been revealed to men will be ready to put their trust in him, because they know what he is like. The Psalmist prays: "For thy name's sake, O Lord, pardon my guilt" (*Psalm* 25: 11), which to all intents and purposes means *for thy love and mercy's sake*. The grounds of the Psalmist's prayer are the character of God as he knows it to be. "For thy name's sake," prays the Psalmist, "lead me, and guide me" (*Psalm* 31: 3). He can bring his request only because he knows the the name—the character—of God. "Some boast of chariots," says the Psalmist, "and some of horses; but we boast of the name of the Lord our God" (*Psalm* 20: 7). Some people put their trust in earthly helps but we will trust God because we know his nature.

So, then, John means that we are assured of forgiveness because we know the character of Jesus Christ. We know that in him we see God. We see in him sacrificial love and patient mercy; therefore we know that God is like that; and, therefore, we can be sure that there is forgiveness for us.

(ii) There is the gift of *increasing knowledge of God*. John no doubt was thinking of his own experience. He was an old man now; he was writing about A.D. 100. For seventy years he had lived with Christ and he had thought about him and come to know him better every day. For the Jew knowledge was not merely an intellectual thing. To know God was not merely to know him as the philosopher knows him; it was to know him as a friend knows him. In Hebrew *to know* is used of the relationship between husband and wife and especially of the sexual act, the most intimate of all relationships (cp. *Genesis* 4: 1). When John spoke of the increasing knowledge of God, he did not mean that the Christian would become an ever more learned theologian; he meant that throughout the years he would become more and more intimately friendly with God.

(iii) There is the *gift of victorious strength*. John looks on the struggle with temptation as a personal struggle. He does not speak in the abstract of conquering evil; he speaks of conquering the Evil One. He sees evil as a personal power which seeks to seduce us from God. Once Robert Louis Stevenson, speaking of an experience which he never told in detail, said, "You know the Caledonian Railway Station in Edinburgh? *Once I met Satan there.*" There can be none of us who has not experienced the attack of the tempter, the personal assault on our virtue and on our loyalty. It is in Christ we receive the power to meet and to defeat this attack. To take a very simple human analogy—we all know that there are some people in whose presence it is easy to be bad and some in whose presence it is necessary to be good. When we walk with Jesus, we are walking with him whose company can enable us to defeat the assaults of the Evil One.

RIVALS FOR THE HUMAN HEART

1 *John* 2: 15–17

> Do not love the world nor the things in the world. If anyone loves the world, the love of the Father is not in him. For everything that is in the world—the flesh's desire, the eye's desire, life's empty pride—does not come from the Father but comes from the world. And the world is passing away, and so is its desire; but he who does God's will abides for ever.

IT was characteristic of ancient thought to see the world in terms of two conflicting principles. We see this very vividly in Zoroastrianism, the religion of the Persians. That was a religion with which the Jews had been brought into contact and which had left a mark upon their thinking. Zoroastrianism saw the world as the battle-ground between the opposing forces of the light and the dark. The god of the light was Ahura-Mazda, the god of the dark was Ahura-Mainyu; and the great decision in life was which side to serve. Every man had to decide to ally himself either with the light or with the dark; that was a conception which the Jews knew well.

But for the Christian the cleavage between the world and the Church had another background. The Jews had for many centuries a basic belief which divided time into two ages, *this present age*, which was wholly evil, and *the age to come*, which was the age of God and, therefore, wholly good. It was a basic belief of the Christian that in Christ the age to come had arrived; the Kingdom of God was here. But the Kingdom of God had not arrived in and for the *world*; it had arrived only in and for the *Church*. Hence the Christian was bound to draw a contrast. The life of the Christian within the Church was the life of the age to come, which was wholly good; on the other hand the world was still living in this present age, which was wholly evil. It followed inevitably that there was a complete cleavage between the Church and the world, and that there could be no fellowship, and even no compromise, between them.

But we must be careful to understand what John meant by the world, the *kosmos*. The Christian did not hate *the world as such*. It was God's creation; and God made all things well. Jesus had loved the beauty of the world; not even Solomon in all his glory was arrayed like one of the scarlet anemones which bloomed for a day and died. Jesus again and again took his illustrations from the world. In that sense the Christian did not hate the world. The earth was not the devil's; the earth was the Lord's and the fullness thereof. But *kosmos* acquired a moral sense. It began to mean *the world apart from God*. C. H. Dodd defines this meaning of *kosmos*: "Our author means human society in so far as it is organized on wrong principles, and characterized by base desires, false values, and egoism." In other words, to John *the world was nothing other than pagan society* with its false values and its false gods.

The world in this passage does not mean the world in general, for God loved the world which he had made; it means the world which, in fact, had forsaken the God who made it.

It so happened that there was a factor in the situation of John's people which made the circumstances even more perilous. It is clear that, although they might be unpopular, they were not undergoing persecution. They were, therefore, under the great and dangerous temptation to compromise with the world. It is always difficult to be different, and it was specially difficult for them.

To this day the Christian cannot escape the obligation to be different from the world. In this passage John sees things as he always sees them—in terms of black and white. As Westcott has it: "There cannot be a vacuum in the soul." This is a matter in which there is no neutrality; a man either loves the world or he loves God, Jesus himself said, "No one can serve two masters" (*Matthew* 6: 24). The ultimate choice remains the same. Are we to accept the world's standards or the standards of God?

THE LIFE IN WHICH THERE IS NO FUTURE

1 *John* 2: 15–17 (*continued*)

JOHN has two things to say about the man who loves the world and compromises with it.

First, he sets out three sins which are typical of the world.

(i) There is the *flesh's desire*. This means far more than what we mean by *sins of the flesh*. To us that expression has to do exclusively with sexual sin. But in the New Testament *the flesh* is that part of our nature which, when it is without the grace of Jesus Christ, offers a bridgehead to sin. It includes the sins of the flesh but also all worldly ambitions and selfish aims. To be subject to the flesh's desire is to judge everything in this world by purely material standards. It is to live a life dominated by the senses. It is to be gluttonous in food; effeminate in luxury; slavish in pleasure; lustful and lax in morals; selfish in the use of possessions; regardless of all the spiritual values; extravagant in the gratification of material desires. The flesh's desire is regardless of the commandments of God, the judgment of God, the standards of God and the very existence of God. We need not think of this as the sin of the gross sinner. Anyone who demands a pleasure which may be the ruin of someone else, anyone who has no respect for the personalities of other people in the gratification of his own desires, anyone who lives in luxury while others live in want, anyone who has made a god of his own comfort and of his own ambition in any part of life, is the servant of the flesh's desire.

(ii) There is the *eye's desire*. This, as C. H. Dodd puts it is "the tendency to be captivated by outward show." It is the spirit which identifies lavish ostentation with real prosperity. It is the spirit which can see nothing without wishing to acquire it and which, having acquired it, flaunts it. It is the spirit which believes that happiness is to be found in the things which money can buy and the eye can see; it has no values other than the material.

(iii) There is *life's empty pride*. Here John uses a most vivid Greek word, *alazoneia*. To the ancient moralists the *alazōn* was the man who laid claims to possessions and to achievements which did not belong to him in order to exalt himself. The *alazōn* is the braggart; and C. H. Dodd calls *alazoneia*, *pretentious egoism*. Theophrastus, the great Greek master of the character study, has a study of the *Alazōn*, he stands in the harbour and boasts of the ships that he has at sea; he ostentatiously sends a messenger to the bank when he has a shilling to his credit; he talks of his friends among the mighty and of the letters he receives from the famous. He details at length his charitable benefactions and his services to the state. All that he occupies is a hired lodging, but he talks of buying a bigger house to match his lavish entertaining. His conversation is a continual boasting about things which he does not possess and all his life is spent in an attempt to impress everyone he meets with his own non-existent importance.

As John sees him, the man of the world is the man who judges everything by his appetites, the man who is the slave of lavish ostentation, the boastful braggart who tries to make himself out a far bigger man than he is.

Then comes John's second warning. The man who attaches himself to the world's aims and the world's ways is giving his life to things which literally have no future. All these things are passing away and none has any permanency. But the man who has taken God as the centre of his life has given himself to the things which last for ever. The man of the world is doomed to disappointment; the man of God is certain of lasting joy.

THE TIME OF THE LAST HOUR

1 *John* 2: 18

> Little children, it is the time of the last hour; and now many anti-christs have risen, just as you heard that Antichrist was to come. That is how we know that it is the time of the last hour.

IT is important that we should understand what John means when he speaks of the time of the last hour. The idea of the last days and of the last hour runs all through the Bible; but there is a most interesting development in its meaning.

(i) The phrase occurs frequently in the very early books of the Old Testament. Jacob, for instance, before his death assembles his sons to tell them what will befall them in the last days (*Genesis* 49: 1; cp. *Numbers* 24: 14). At that time the last days were when the people of Israel would enter into the Promised Land, and would at last enter into full enjoyment of the promised blessings of God.

(ii) The phrase frequently occurs in the prophets. In the last days the mountain of the Lord shall be established as the highest of the mountains, and shall be raised above the hills, and all nations shall flow to it (*Isaiah* 2: 2; *Micah* 4: 1). In the last days God's Holy City will be supreme; and Israel will render to God the perfect obedience which is his due (cp. *Jeremiah* 23: 20; 30: 24; 48: 47). In the last days there will be the supremacy of God and the obedience of his people.

(iii) In the Old Testament itself, and in the times between

the Old and the New Testaments, the last days become associated with the Day of the Lord. No conception is more deeply interwoven into Scripture than this. The Jews had come to believe that all time was divided into two ages. In between *this present age*, which was wholly evil, and *the age to come*, which was the golden time of God's supremacy there was the Day of the Lord, the last days, which would be a time of terror, of cosmic dissolution and of judgment, the birthpangs of the new age.

The last hour does not mean a time of annihilation whose end will be a great nothingness as there was at the beginning. In biblical thought the last time is the end of one age and the beginning of another. It is *last* in the sense that things as they are pass away; but it leads not to world obliteration but to world re-creation.

Here is the centre of the matter. The question then becomes: "Will a man be wiped out in the judgment of the old or will he enter into the glory of the new?" That is the alternative with which John—like all the biblical writers—is confronting men. Men have the choice of allying themselves with the old world, which is doomed to dissolution, or of allying themselves with Christ and entering into the new world, the very world of God. Here lies the urgency. If it was a simple matter of utter obliteration, no one could do anything about it. But it is a matter of re-creation, and whether a man will enter the new world or not depends on whether or not he gives his life to Jesus Christ.

In fact John was wrong. It was not the last hour for his people. Eighteen hundred years have gone by and the world still exists. Does the whole conception, then, belong to a sphere of thought which must be discarded? The answer is that in this conception there is an eternal relevance. *Every hour is the last hour*. In the world there is a continual conflict between good and evil, between God and that which is anti-God. And in every moment and in every decision a man is confronted with the choice of allying himself either with God or with the evil forces which are against God; and of thereby ensuring, or failing to ensure, his own share in eternal life. The conflict between good and evil never stops; therefore, the choice never stops; therefore, in a very real sense every hour is the last hour.

THE ANTICHRIST

1 *John* 2: 18 (*continued*)

IN this verse we meet the conception of *Antichrist*. *Antichrist* is a word which occurs only in John's letters in the New Testament (1 *John* 2: 22; 4: 3; 2 *John* 7); but it is the expression of an idea which is as old as religion itself.

From its derivation *Antichrist* can have two meanings. *Anti* is a Greek preposition which can mean either *against* or *in place of*. *Stratēgos* is the Greek word for a *commander*, and *antistratēgos* can mean either *the hostile commander* or the *deputy commander*. *Antichrist* can mean either the opponent of Christ or the one who seeks to put himself in the place of Christ. In this case the meaning will come to the same thing, but with this difference. If we take the meaning to be *the one who is opposed to Christ*, the opposition is plain. If we take the meaning to be *the one who seeks to put himself in the place of Christ*, Antichrist can be one who subtly tries to take the place of Christ from within the church and the Christian community. The one will be an open opposition; the other a subtle infiltration. We need not choose between these meanings, for Antichrist can act in either way.

The simplest way to think of it is that Christ is the incarnation of God and goodness, and Antichrist is the incarnation of the devil and evil.

We began by saying that this is an idea which is as old as religion itself; men have always felt that in the universe there is a power which is in opposition to God. One of its earliest forms occurs in the Babylonian legend of creation. According to it there was in the very beginning a primaeval sea monster called Tiamat; this sea monster was subdued by Marduk but not killed; it was only asleep and the final battle was still to come. That mythical idea of the primaeval monster occurs in the Old Testament again and again. There the monster is often called Rahab or the crooked serpent or leviathan. "Thou didst crush Rahab like a carcass," says the Psalmist (*Psalm* 89: 10). "His hand pierced the fleeing serpent," says Job (*Job* 26: 13). Isaiah speaking of the arm of the Lord, says, "Was it not thou that didst cut Rahab in pieces, that didst pierce the dragon?" (*Isaiah* 51: 9). Isaiah writes: "In that day the Lord with his hard and great and strong sword will punish leviathan the fleeing serpent, leviathan the twisting serpent, and he will slay the dragon that is in the sea" (*Isaiah* 27: 1). All these are references to the primaeval dragon. This idea is obviously one which belongs to the childhood of mankind and its basis is that in the universe there is a power hostile to God.

Originally this power was conceived of as the dragon. Inevitably as time went on it became personalized. Every time there arose a very evil man who seemed to be setting himself against God and bent on the obliteration of his people, the tendency was to identify him with this anti-God force. For instance, about 168 B.C. there emerged the figure of Antiochus Epiphanes, King of Syria. He resolved on a deliberate attempt to eliminate Judaism from this earth. He invaded Jerusalem, killed thousands of Jews, and sold tens of thousands into slavery. To circumcise a child or to own a copy of the Law was made a crime punishable by instant death. In the Temple courts was erected a great altar to Zeus. Swine's flesh was offered on it. The Temple chambers were made into public brothels. Here was a cold-blooded effort to wipe out the Jewish religion. It was Antiochus whom Daniel called "The abomination that makes desolate" (*Daniel* 11: 31; 12: 11). Here men thought was the anti-God force become flesh.

It was this same phrase that men took in the days of Mark's gospel when they talked of "The Abomination of Desolation"—"The Appalling Horror," as Moffatt translates it—being set up in the Temple (*Mark* 13: 14; *Matthew* 24: 15).

Here the reference was to Caligula, the more than half-mad Roman Emperor, who wished to set up his own image in the Holy of Holies in the Temple. It was felt that this was the act of anti-God incarnate.

In 2 *Thessalonians* 2:3, 4, Paul speaks of "the man of sin," the one who exalts himself above all that is called God and all that is worshipped and who sets himself up in the very Temple of God. We do not know whom Paul was expecting, but again there is this thought of one who was the incarnation of everything which was opposed to God.

In *Revelation* there is the beast (13:1; 16:13; 19:20; 20:10). Here is very probably another figure. Nero was regarded by all as a human monster. His excesses disgusted the Romans and his savage persecution tortured the Christians. In due time he died; but he had been so wicked that men could not believe that he was really dead. And so there arose the *Nero Redivivus*, Nero resurrected, legend, which said that Nero was not dead but had gone to Parthia and would come with the Parthian hordes to descend upon men. He is the beast, the Antichrist, the incarnation of evil.

All down history there have been these identifications of human figures with Antichrist. The Pope, Napoleon, Mussolini, Hitler, have all in their day received this iden-tification.

But the fact is that Antichrist is not so much a person as a principle, the principle which is actively opposed to God and which may well be thought of as incarnating itself in those men in every generation who have seemed to be the blatant opponents of God.

THE BATTLE OF THE MIND

1 *John* 2:18 (*continued*)

JOHN has a view of Antichrist which is characteristically his own. To him the sign that Antichrist is in the world is the false belief and the dangerous teaching of the heretics. The

Church had been well forewarned that in the last days false teachers would come. Jesus had said, "Many will come in my name, saying, I am he; and they will lead many astray" (*Mark* 13: 6; cp. *Matthew* 24: 5). Before he left them, Paul had warned his Ephesian friends: "After my departure fierce wolves will come in among you, not sparing the flock. And from among your own selves will arise men, speaking perverse things, to draw away the disciples after them" (*Acts* 20: 29, 30). The situation which had been foretold had now arisen.

But John had a special view of this situation. He did not think of Antichrist as one single individual figure but rather as a power of falsehood speaking in and through the false teachers. Just as the Holy Spirit was inspiring the true teachers and the true prophets, so there was an evil spirit inspiring the false teachers and the false prophets.

The great interest and relevance of this is that for John *the battleground was in the mind*. The spirit of Antichrist was struggling with the Spirit of God for the possession of men's minds. What makes this so significant is that we can see exactly this process at work today. Men have brought the indoctrination of the human mind to a science. We see men take an idea and repeat it and repeat it and repeat it until it settles into the minds of others and they begin to accept it as true simply because they have heard it so often. This is easier today than ever it was with so many means of mass communication—books, newspapers, wireless, television, and the vast resources of modern advertising. A skilled propagandist can take an idea and infiltrate it into men's minds until, all unaware, they are indoctrinated with it. We do not say that John foresaw all this but he did see the mind as the field of operations for Antichrist. He no longer thought in terms of a single demonic figure but in terms of a force of evil deliberately seeking to pervade men's minds; and there is nothing more potent for evil than that.

If there is one special task which confronts the Church today, it is to learn how to use the power of the media of mass communication to counteract the evil ideas with which the minds of men are being deliberately indoctrinated.

THE SIFTING OF THE CHURCH

1 *John* 2: 19–21

They have gone out from among us but they are not of our number. If they had been of our number, they would have remained with us. But things have happened as they have happened, that it may be clearly demonstrated that all of them are not of us. But you have received anointing from the Holy One and you all possess knowledge. I have not written this letter to you because you do not know the truth, but because you do know it and because no lie comes from the truth.

As things have turned out, John sees in the Church a time of sifting. The false teachers had voluntarily left the Christian fellowship; and that fact had shown that they did not really belong there. They were aliens and their own conduct had shown it to be so.

The last phrase of verse 19 can have two meanings.

(i) It may mean, as in our translation: "All of them are not of us," or, as we might better put it, "None of them are from us." That is to say, however attractive some of them may be and however fine their teaching sounds, they are all alike alien to the Church.

(ii) It is just possible that what the phrase means is that these men have gone out from the Church to make it clear that "all who are in the Church do not really belong to it." As C. H. Dodd puts it: "Membership of the Church is no guarantee that a man belongs to Christ and not to Antichrist." As A. E. Brooke puts it—although he does not agree that it is the meaning of the Greek—"External membership is no proof of inward union." As Paul had it: "For not all who are descended from Israel belong to Israel" (*Romans* 9: 6).

A time such as had come upon John's people had its value, for it sifted the false from the true.

In verse 20 John goes on to remind his people that all of them possess knowledge. The people who had gone out were Gnostics who claimed that there had been given to them a secret, special and advanced knowledge which was not open to the ordinary Christian. John reminds his people that in matters of faith the humblest Christian need have no feeling of inferiority to the most learned scholar. There are, of course, matters of technical scholarship, of language, of history, which must be the preserve of the expert; but the essentials of the faith are the possession of every man.

This leads John to his last point in this section. He writes to them, not because they did not know the truth, but because they did. Westcott puts it in this way: "The object of the apostle in writing was not to communicate fresh knowledge, but to bring into active and decisive use the knowledge which his readers already possessed." The greatest Christian defence is simply to remember what we know. What we need is not new truth, but that the truth which we already know become active and effective in our lives.

This is an approach which Paul continually uses. He writes to the Thessalonians: "But concerning love of the brethren you have no need to have any one write to you, for you yourselves have been taught by God to love one another" (1 *Thessalonians* 4: 9). What they need is not new truth but to put into practice the truth they already know. He writes to the Romans: "I myself, am satisfied about you, my brethren, that you yourselves are full of goodness, filled with all knowledge, and able to instruct one another. But on some points I have written to you very boldly by way of reminder, because of the grace given me by God" (*Romans* 15: 14, 15). What they need is not so much to be taught as to be reminded.

It is the simple fact of the Christian life that things would be different at once if we would only put into practice what we already know. That is not to say that we never need to learn anything new; but it is to say that, even as we are, we have light enough to walk by if we would only use it.

THE MASTER LIE

1 *John* 2: 22, 23

> Who is the liar but the man who denies that Jesus is the Anointed One of God? Antichrist is he who denies the Father and the Son. Anyone who denies the Son does not even have the Father; and everyone who acknowledges the Son has the Father also.

As someone has put it, to deny that Jesus is the Christ is the master lie, the lie *par excellence*; the lie of all lies.

John says that he who denies the Son has not the Father either. What lies behind that saying is this. The false teachers pleaded, "It may be that we have different ideas from yours about *Jesus*; but you and we do believe the same things about *God*." John's answer is that that is an impossible position; no man can deny the Son and still have the Father. How does he arrive at this view?

He arrives at it because no one who accepts New Testament teaching can arrive at any other. It is the consistent teaching of the New Testament and it is the claim of Jesus himself that apart from him no man can know God. Jesus said quite clearly that no man knows the Father except the Son and him to whom the Son reveals that knowledge (*Matthew* 11: 27; *Luke* 10: 22). Jesus said, "He who believes in me, believes not in me but in him who sent me. And he who sees me sees him who sent me" (*John* 12: 44, 45). When, toward the end, Philip said that they would be content if Jesus would only show them the Father, Jesus's answer was: "He who has seen me has seen the Father" (*John* 14: 6–9). It is through Jesus that men know God; it is in Jesus that men can approach God. If we deny Jesus's right to speak, if we deny his special knowledge and his special relationship to God, we can have no more confidence in what he says. His words become no more than the guesses which any good and great man could make. Apart from Jesus we have no secure knowledge of God; to deny him is at the same time to lose all grip of God.

Further, it is Jesus's claim that a man's reaction to him is, in fact, a reaction to God and that that reaction settles his destiny in time and in eternity. He said, "So everyone who acknowledges me before men, I also will acknowledge before my Father who is in heaven; but whoever denies me before men, I also will deny before my Father who is in heaven" (*Matthew* 10: 32, 33). To deny Jesus is to be separated from God, for on our reaction to Jesus our relationship to God depends.

To deny Jesus is indeed the *master lie*, for it is to lose entirely the faith and the knowledge which he alone makes possible.

We may say that there are three New Testament confessions of Jesus. There is the confession that he is the *Son of God* (*Matthew* 16: 16; *John* 9: 35–38); there is the confession that he is *Lord* (*Philippians* 2: 11); and there is the confession that he is *Messiah* (1 *John* 2: 22). The essence of every one of them is the affirmation that Jesus stands in a unique relationship to God; and to deny that relationship is to deny the certainty that everything Jesus said about God is true. The Christian faith depends on the unique relationship of Jesus to God. John is, therefore, right; the man who denies the Son has lost the Father, too.

THE UNIVERSAL PRIVILEGE

1 *John* 2: 24–29

If that which you have heard from the beginning remains within you, you too will remain in the Son and in the Father. And this is the promise which he made to you—eternal life. I am writing these things to you to warn you about those who are seeking to lead you astray. As for you, if that anointing which you have received from him remains in you, you have no need for anyone to

teach you. But, as his anointing teaches you about all things and
is true and is no lie, and as he has taught you, remain in him.
And now, little children, remain in him, so that, if he appears, we
may have confidence and not shrink in shame away from him at his
coming. If you know that he is righteous, you must be aware that
everyone who does righteousness is born of him.

JOHN is pleading with his people to abide in the things which
they have learned, for, if they do, they will abide in Christ.
The great interest of this passage lies in an expression which
John has already used. In verse 20 he has already spoken of
the *anointing* which his people had had from the Holy One
and through which all of them were equipped with knowledge.
Here he speaks of the anointing which they have received and
the anointing which teaches them all things. What is the
thought behind this word *anointing*? We shall have to go back
some distance in Hebrew thought to get at it.

In Hebrew thought and practice anointing was connected
with three kinds of people. (i) *Priests* were anointed. The
ritual regulation runs: "You shall take the anointing oil, and
pour it on his (the priest's) head and anoint him" (*Exodus*
29: 7; cp. 40: 13; *Leviticus* 16: 32). (ii) *Kings* were anointed.
Samuel anointed Saul as king of the nation (1 *Samuel* 9: 16;
10: 1). Later, Samuel anointed David as king (1 *Samuel* 16: 3,
12). Elijah was bidden to anoint Hazael and Jehu (1 *Kings*
19: 15, 16). Anointing was the symbol of coronation, as it
still is. (iii) *Prophets* were anointed. Elijah was bidden to
anoint Elisha as his successor (1 *Kings* 19: 16). The Lord had
anointed the prophet Isaiah to bring good tidings to the nation
(*Isaiah* 61: 1).

Here, then, is the first significant thing. In the old days
anointing had been the privilege of the chosen few, the priests,
the prophets and the kings; but now it is the privilege of
every Christian, however humble he may be. First, then, the
anointing stands for the privilege of the Christian in Jesus
Christ.

The High Priest was called *The Anointed*; but the supreme
Anointed One was the *Messiah*. (*Messiah* is the Hebrew for

The Anointed One and *Christos* is the Greek equivalent). So Jesus was supremely *The Anointed One*. The question then arose: when was he anointed? The answer which the Church always gave was that *at his baptism* Jesus was anointed with the Holy Spirit (*Acts* 10: 38).

The Greek world also knew of anointing. Anointing was one of the ceremonies of initiation into the Mystery Religions in which a man was supposed to gain special knowledge of God. We know that some at least of the false teachers claimed a special anointing which brought them a special knowledge of God. Hippolytus tells us how these false teachers said, "We alone of all men are Christians, who complete the mystery at the third portal and are anointed there with speechless anointing." John's answer is that it is the ordinary Christian who has the only true anointing, the anointing which Jesus gives.

When did that anointing come to the Christian and of what does it consist?

The first question is easy to answer. There was only one ceremony that all Christians passed through, and that was *baptism*; it was, indeed, in later days the standard practice at baptism to anoint Christians with holy oil, as Tertullian tells us.

The second question is not so easy. There are, in fact, two equally possible answers.

(i) It may be that the anointing means the coming of the Spirit upon the Christian in baptism. In the early Church that happened in the most visible way (*Acts* 8: 17). If in this passage we were to substitute the *Holy Spirit* for anointing we would get excellent sense.

(ii) But there is another possibility. Verses 24 and 27 are almost exactly parallel in expression. In verse 24 we read: "Let what you have heard from the beginning abide in you." And in verse 27 we read: "But the anointing which you received from him abides in you." *That which you have received from the beginning* and *the anointing* are exactly parallel. Therefore, it may well be that the anointing which the Christian

receives is the instruction in the Christian faith which is given
him when he enters the Church.

It may well be that we do not need to choose between
these two interpretations and that they are both present.
This would mean something very valuable. It would mean that
we have two tests by which to judge any new teaching
offered to us. (i) Is it in accordance with the Christian
tradition which we have been taught? (ii) Is it in accordance
with the witness of the Holy Spirit speaking within?

Here are the Christian criteria of truth. There is an *external*
test. All teaching must be in accordance with the tradition
handed down to us in Scripture and in the Church. There is
an *internal* test. All teaching must undergo the test of the
Holy Spirit witnessing within our hearts.

ABIDING IN CHRIST

1 *John* 2: 24-29 (*continued*)

BEFORE we leave this passage we must note two great and
practical things in it.

(i) In verse 28, John urges his people to abide continually
in Christ so that, when he does come back in power and
glory, they may not shrink from him in shame. By far the
best way to be ready for the coming of Christ is to live with
him every day. If we do that, his coming will be no shock to
us but simply the entry into the nearer presence of one with
whom we have lived for long.

Even if we have doubts and difficulties about the physical
Second Coming of Christ, this still remains true. For every
man life will some day come to an end; God's summons
comes to all to rise and bid this world farewell. If we have
never thought of God and if Jesus has been but a dim and
distant memory, that will be a summons to voyage into a
frightening unknown. But if we have lived consciously in the
presence of Christ, if day by day we have talked and walked

with God, that will be a summons to come home and to enter into the nearer presence of one who is not a stranger but a friend.

(ii) In verse 29 John comes back to a thought which is never far from his mind. The only way in which a man can prove that he is abiding in Christ is by the righteousness of his life. The profession a man makes will always be proved or disproved by his practice.

REMEMBER THE PRIVILEGES OF THE CHRISTIAN LIFE

1 *John* 3: 1, 2

See what kind of love the Father has given to us, that we should be called the children of God—and such we indeed are. The reason why the world does not recognize us is that it did not recognize him. Beloved, even as things are we are children of God, and it has not yet been made clear what we shall be. We know that, if it shall be made clear, we shall be like him because we shall see him as he is.

IT may well be that the best illumination of this passage is the Scottish Paraphrase of it:

> Behold the amazing gift of love
> the Father hath bestow'd
> On us, the sinful sons of men,
> to call us sons of God!
>
> Concealed as yet this honour lies,
> by this dark world unknown,
> A world that knew not when he came,
> even God's eternal Son.
>
> High is the rank we now possess,
> but higher we shall rise;
> Though what we shall hereafter be
> is hid from mortal eyes.

Our souls, we know, when he appears,
　shall bear his image bright;
For all his glory, full disclosed,
　shall open to our sight.

A hope so great, and so divine,
　may trials well endure;
And purge the soul from sense and sin,
　as Christ himself is pure.

John begins by demanding that his people should remember
their privileges. It is their privilege that they are called *the
children of God*. There is something even in a name. Chryso-
stom, in a sermon on how to bring up children, advises
parents to give their boy some great scriptural name, to teach
him repeatedly the story of the original bearer of the name,
and so to give him a standard to live up to when he grows
to manhood. So the Christian has the privilege of being called
the child of God. Just as to belong to a great school, a
great regiment, a great church, a great household is an inspiration to fine living, so, even more, to bear the name of
the family of God is something to keep a man's feet on the
right way and to set him climbing.

But, as John points out, we are not merely *called* the
children of God; we *are* the children of God.

There is something here which we may well note. It is by
the gift of God that a man becomes a child of God. By
nature a man is the *creature* of God, but it is by grace that
he *becomes* the child of God. There are two English words
which are closely connected but whose meanings are widely
different, *paternity* and *fatherhood*. *Paternity* describes a relationship in which a man is responsible for the physical
existence of a child; *fatherhood* describes an intimate, loving,
relationship. In the sense of *paternity* all men are children
of God; but in the sense of *fatherhood* men are children of
God only when he makes his gracious approach to them and
they respond.

There are two pictures, one from the Old Testament and one

from the New, which aptly and vividly set out this relationship. In the Old Testament there is the *covenant idea*. Israel is the covenant people of God. That is to say, God on his own initiative had made a special approach to Israel; he was to be uniquely their God, and they were to be uniquely his people. As an integral part of the covenant God gave to Israel his law, and it was on the keeping of that law that the covenant relationship depended.

In the New Testament there is the idea of *adoption* (*Romans* 8: 14–17; 1 *Corinthians* 1: 9; *Galatians* 3: 26, 27; 4: 6, 7). Here is the idea that by a deliberate act of adoption on the part of God the Christian enters into his family.

While all men are children of God in the sense that they owe their lives to him, they become his children in the intimate and loving sense of the term only by an act of God's initiating grace and the response of their own hearts.

Immediately the question arises: if men have that great honour when they become Christians, why are they so despised by the world? The answer is that they are experiencing only what Jesus Christ has already experienced. When he came into the world, he was not recognized as the Son of God; the world preferred its own ideas and rejected his. The same is bound to happen to any man who chooses to embark on the way of Jesus Christ.

REMEMBER THE POSSIBILITIES OF
THE CHRISTIAN LIFE

1 *John* 3: 1, 2 (*continued*)

JOHN, then, begins by reminding his people of the privileges of the Christian life. He goes on to set before them what is in many ways a still more tremendous truth, the great fact that *this life is only a beginning*. Here John observes the only true agnosticism. So great is the future and its glory that he will not even guess at it or try to put it into inevitably inadequate words. But there are certain things he does say about it.

(i) When Christ appears in his glory, we shall be like him. Surely in John's mind there was the saying of the old creation story that man was made in the image and in the likeness of God (*Genesis* 1: 26). That was God's intention; and that was man's destiny. We have only to look into any mirror to see how far man has fallen short of that destiny. But John believes that in Christ a man will finally attain it, and at last bear the image and the likeness of God. It is John's belief that only through the work of Christ in his soul can a man reach the true manhood God meant him to reach.

(ii) When Christ appears, we shall see him and be like him. The goal of all the great souls has been the vision of God. The end of all devotion is to see God. But that vision of God is not for the sake of intellectual satisfaction; it is in order that we may become like him. There is a paradox here. We cannot become like God unless we see him; and we cannot see him unless we are pure in heart, for only the pure in heart shall see God (*Matthew* 5: 8). In order to see God, we need the purity which only he can give. We are not to think of this vision of God as something which only the great mystics can enjoy. There is somewhere the story of a poor and simple man who would often go into a cathedral to pray; and he would always pray kneeling before the crucifix. Someone noticed that, though he knelt in the attitude of prayer, his lips never moved and he never seemed to say anything. He asked what he was doing kneeling like that and the man answered: "I look at him; and he looks at me." That is the vision of God in Christ that the simplest soul can have; and he who looks long enough at Jesus Christ must become like him.

One other thing we must note. John is here thinking in terms of the Second Coming of Christ. It may be that we can think in the same terms; or it may be that we cannot think so literally of a coming of Christ in glory. Be that as it may, there will come for every one of us the day when

we shall see Christ and behold his glory. Here there is always
the veil of sense and time, but the day will come when that
veil, too, will be torn in two.

> When death these mortal eyes shall seal,
>   And still this throbbing heart,
> The rending veil shall thee reveal
>   All glorious as thou art.

Therein is the Christian hope and the vast possibility of the
Christian life.

THE OBLIGATION OF PURITY

1 *John* 3: 3–8

Anyone who rests this hope on him purifies himself as he is pure.
Anyone who commits sin commits lawlessness, and sin is lawlessness. And you know that he appeared that he might take away our
sins and there is no sin in him. Anyone who abides in him does
not sin. Anyone who sins has not seen him, and does not know
him. Little children, let no one deceive you. He who does
righteousness is righteous, even as he is righteous. He who does
sin is of the devil, because the devil is a sinner from the beginning. The purpose for which the Son of God appeared was that
he might destroy the works of the devil.

JOHN has just said that the Christian is on the way to seeing
God and being like him. There is nothing like a great aim
for helping a man to resist temptation. A novelist draws the
picture of a young man who always refused to share in the
lower pleasures to which his comrades often invited and even
urged him. His explanation was that some day something
fine was going to come to him, and he must keep himself
ready for it. The man who knows that God is at the end
of the road will make all life a preparation to meet him.

This passage is directed against the Gnostic false teachers.
As we have seen they produced more than one reason to
justify sin. They said that the body was evil and that, therefore,

there was no harm in sating its lusts, because what happened to it was of no importance. They said that the truly spiritual man was so armoured with the Spirit that he could sin to his heart's content and take no harm from it. They even said that the true Gnostic was under obligation both to scale the heights and to plumb the depths so that he might be truly said to know all things. Behind John's answer there is a kind of analysis of sin.

He begins by insisting that no one is superior to the moral law. No one can say that it is quite safe for him to allow himself certain things, although they may be dangerous for others. As A. E. Brooke puts it: "The test of progress is obedience." Progress does not confer the privilege to sin; the further on a man is the more disciplined a character he will be. John goes on to imply certain basic truths about sin.

(i) He tells us *what sin is*. It is the deliberate breaking of a law which a man well knows. Sin is to obey oneself rather than to obey God.

(ii) He tells us *what sin does*. It undoes the work of Christ. Christ is the Lamb of God who takes away the sins of the world (*John* 1: 29). To sin is to bring back what he came into the world to abolish.

(iii) He tells us *why sin is*. It comes from the failure to abide in Christ. We need not think that this is a truth only for advanced mystics. It simply means this—so long as we remember the continual presence of Jesus, we will not sin; it is when we forget that presence that we sin.

(iv) He tells us *whence sin comes*. It comes from the devil; and the devil is he who sins, as it were, on principle. That probably is the meaning of the phrase *from the beginning* (verse 8). We sin for the pleasure that we think it will bring to us; the devil sins as a matter of principle. The New Testament does not try to explain the devil and his origin; but it is quite convinced—and it is a fact of universal experience—that in the world there is a power hostile to God; and to sin is to obey that power instead of God.

(v) He tells us how *sin is conquered*. It is conquered because

Jesus Christ destroyed the works of the devil. The New
Testament often dwells on the Christ who faced and conquered the powers of evil (*Matthew* 12: 25–29; *Luke* 10: 18;
Colossians 2: 15; 1 *Peter* 3: 22; *John* 12: 31). He has broken
the power of evil, and by his help that same victory can
be ours.

THE MAN WHO IS BORN OF GOD

1 *John* 3: 9

> Anyone who has been born of God does not commit sin, because
> his seed abides in him; and he cannot be a consistent and
> deliberate sinner, because he has been born of God.

THIS verse bristles with difficulties, and yet it is obviously
of the first importance to find out what it means.

First, what does John mean by the phrase: "*Because his
seed abides in him*"? There are three possibilities.

(i) Frequently the Bible uses the word *seed* to mean a man's
family and descendants. Abraham and his *seed* are to keep
the covenant of God (*Genesis* 17: 9). God made his promise
to Abraham and to his *seed* for ever (*Luke* 1: 55). The Jews
claim to be Abraham's *seed* (*John* 8: 33, 37). In *Galatians* 3,
Paul speaks about Abraham's *seed* (*Galatians* 3: 16, 29). If we
take *seed* in that sense here, we need to take *him* as referring
to God and then we get very good sense. "Anyone who has
been born of God does not sin, because God's family constantly abide in God." God's family live so near to God
that they may be said to abide in him. The man who lives
like that has a strong defence against sin.

(ii) It is human seed which produces human life, and the
child may be said to have his father's seed in him. Now
the Christian is reborn through God and, therefore, has God's
seed in him. This was an idea with which the people of
John's age were very familiar. The Gnostics said that God
had sowed seeds into this world and through the action of

these seeds the world was being perfected; and they claimed that it was the true Gnostics who had received these seeds. Some Gnostics said that man's body was a material and evil thing; but into some bodies Wisdom secretly sowed seeds and the truly spiritual men have these seeds of God for souls. This was closely connected with the Stoic belief that God was fiery spirit and a man's soul, that which gave him life and reason, was a spark (*scintilla*) of that divine fire which had come from God to reside in a man's body.

If we take John's words this way, it means that every reborn man has the seed of God in him, and that, therefore, he cannot sin. There is no doubt that John's readers would know this idea.

(iii) There is a much simpler idea. Twice at least in the New Testament *the word of God* is that which is said to bring rebirth to men. James has it: "Of his own will he brought us forth by the word of truth that we should be a kind of first fruits of his creatures" (*James* 1: 18). The word of God is like the seed of God which produces new life. Peter has this idea even more clearly, "You have been born anew, not of perishable seed but of imperishable, through the living and abiding word of God" (1 *Peter* 1: 23). There *the word of God* is definitely identified with *the imperishable seed of God*. If we take it this way, John means that the man who is born of God cannot sin because he has the strength and guidance of the word of God within him. This third way is simplest and, on the whole best. The Christian is preserved from sin by the indwelling power of the word of God.

THE MAN WHO CANNOT SIN

1 *John* 3: 9 (*continued*)

SECOND, this verse presents us with the problem of relating it with certain other things which John has already said about sin. Let us set the verse down, as it is in the Revised Standard Version:

> No one born of God commits sin; for God's nature abides in him, and he cannot sin because he is born of God.

Taken at its face value this means that it is impossible for the man who is born of God to sin. Now John has already said, "if we say we have no sin, we deceive ourselves, and the truth is not in us"; and "if we say that we have not sinned, we make God a liar"; and he urges us to confess our sins (1 *John* 1: 8–10). He goes on to say, "if we do sin, we have an advocate with the Father in the person of Jesus Christ." On the face of it there is contradiction here. In the one place John is saying that man cannot be anything other than a sinner and that, there is an atonement for his sin. In the other place he is saying equally definitely that the man who is born of God cannot sin. What is the explanation?

(i) John thinks in Jewish categories because he could do no other. We have already seen that he knew and accepted the Jewish picture of the two ages, *this present age* and *the age to come*. We have also seen that it was John's belief that, whatever the world was like, Christians by virtue of the work of Christ had already entered into the new age. It was exactly one of the characteristics of the new age that those who lived in it would be free from sin. In *Enoch* we read: "Then too will wisdom be bestowed on the elect, and they will all live and *never again sin*, either through heedlessness or through pride" (*Enoch* 5: 8). If that is true of the new age, it ought to be true of Christians who are living in it. But, in fact, it is still not true because Christians have not even yet escaped from the power of sin. We might then say that in this passage John is setting down the *ideal* of what should be and in the other two passages he is facing the *actuality* of what is. We might put it that he knows the ideal and confronts men with it; but also faces the facts and sees the cure in Christ for them.

(ii) That may well be so but there is more to it. In the

Greek there is a subtle difference in tenses which makes a very wide difference in meaning. In 1 *John* 2: 1 it is John's injunction *that you may not sin*. In that verse *sin* is in the *aorist* tense which indicates a particular and definite act. So what John is saying is quite clearly that Christians must not commit individual acts of sin; but if they do lapse into sin, they have in Christ an advocate to plead their cause and a sacrifice to atone. On the other hand, in our present passage in both cases *sin* is in the *present* tense and indicates habitual action.

What John is saying may be put down in four stages. (*a*) The ideal is that in the new age sin is gone for ever. (*b*) Christians must try to make that true and with the help of Christ struggle to avoid individual acts of sin. (*c*) In fact all men have these lapses and when they do, they must humbly confess them to God, who will always forgive the penitent heart. (*d*) In spite of that, no Christian can possibly be a deliberate and consistent sinner; no Christian can live a life in which sin is dominant in all his actions.

John is not setting before us a terrifying perfectionism; but he is demanding a life which is ever on the watch against sin, a life in which sin is not the normal accepted way but the abnormal moment of defeat. John is not saying that the man who abides in God cannot sin; but he is saying that the man who abides in God cannot continue to be a deliberate sinner.

THE MARKS OF THE CHILDREN OF GOD

1 *John* 3: 10–18

In this the children of God and the children of the devil are made plain; anyone who does not do righteousness is not of God, and neither is he who does not love his brother, because the message that we have heard from the beginning is the message that we should love one another, that we should not be like Cain, who was of the Evil One and slew his brother. And why did he slay him? Because his works were evil and his brother's works were just. Do not be surprised, brothers, if the world hates you. We know that we have passed from death to life, because we love the brothers. He who does not love remains in death. Anyone who hates his brother is a murderer. He does not possess eternal life abiding within him. In this we recognize his love, that he laid down his life for us; and we ought to lay down our life for the brothers. Whoever possesses enough for his livelihood in this world and sees his brother in need and shuts his heart against him, how does the love of God abide in him? My dear children, do not make love a matter of talking and of the tongue, but love in deed and in truth.

THIS is a passage with a closely-knit argument and a kind of parenthesis in the middle.

As Westcott has it: "Life reveals the children of God." There is no way of telling what a tree is other than by its fruits, and there is no way of telling what a man is other than by his conduct. John lays it down that any one who does not do righteousness is thereby demonstrated to be not of God. At present we shall omit the parenthesis and go straight on with the argument.

Although John is a mystic, he has a very practical mind; and, therefore, he will not leave righteousness vague and undefined. Someone might say, "Very well, I accept the fact that the only thing which proves that a man belongs to God is the righteousness of his life. But what is righteousness?" John's answer is clear and unequivocal. *To be righteous is to love our brother men.* That, says John, is a duty about which we should never be in any doubt. And he goes on to adduce various reasons why that commandment is so central and so binding.

(i) It is a duty which has been inculcated into the Christian from the first moment that he entered the Church. The Christian ethic can be summed up in the one word love and from the moment that a man pledges himself to Christ, he pledges himself to make love the mainspring of his life.

(ii) For that very reason the fact that a man loves his

brother men is the final proof that he has passed from death
to life. As A. E. Brooke puts it: "Life is a chance of learn-
ing how to love." Life without love is death. To love is to be
in the light; to hate is to remain in the dark. We need no
further proof of that than to look at the face of a man who
is in love and the face of a man who is full of hate; it will
show the glory or the blackness in his heart.

(iii) Further, not to love is to become a murderer. There
can be no doubt that John is thinking of the words of
Jesus in the Sermon on the Mount (*Matthew* 5: 21, 22). Jesus
said that the old law forbade murder but the new law declared
that anger and bitterness and contempt were just as serious
sins. Whenever there is hatred in the heart a man becomes
a potential murderer. To allow hatred to settle in the heart
is to break a definite commandment of Jesus. Therefore, the
man who loves is a follower of Christ and the man who
hates is no follower of his.

(iv) There follows still another step in this closely-knit
argument. A man may say, "I admit this obligation of love
and I will try to fulfil it; but I do not know what it involves."
John's answer (verse 16) is: "If you want to see what this love
is, look at Jesus Christ. In his death for men on the Cross
it is fully displayed." In other words, the Christian life is the
imitation of Christ. "Have this mind among yourselves, which
you have in Christ Jesus" (*Philippians* 2: 5). "He left us an
example that we should follow in his steps" (1 *Peter* 2: 21).
No man can look at Christ and then say that he does not
know what the Christian life is.

(v) John meets one more possible objection. A man may say,
"How can I follow in the steps of Christ? He laid down
his life upon the Cross. You say I ought to lay down my life
for the brothers. But opportunities so dramatic as that do not
come into my life. What then?" John's answer is: "True. But
when you see your brother in need and you have enough,
to give to him of what you have is to follow Christ. To
shut your heart and to refuse to give is to show that that
love of God which was in Jesus Christ has no place in you."

John insists that we can find plenty of opportunities to show forth the love of Christ in the life of the every day. C. H. Dodd writes finely on this passage: "There were occasions in the life of the early church, as there are certainly tragic occasions at the present day, for a quite literal obedience to this precept (i.e., to lay down our life for the brothers). But not all life is tragic; and yet the same principle of conduct must apply all through. Thus it may call for the simple expenditure of money we might have spent upon ourselves, to relieve the need of someone poorer. It is, after all, the same principle of action, though at a lower level of intensity: it is the willingness to surrender that which has value for our own life, to enrich the life of another. If such a minimum response to the law of charity, called for by such an everyday situation, is absent, then it is idle to pretend we are within the family of God, the realm in which love is operative as the principle and the token of eternal life."

Fine words will never take the place of fine deeds; and no amount of talk of Christian love will take the place of a kindly action to a man in need, involving some self-sacrifice, for in that action the principle of the Cross is operative again.

THE WORLD'S RESENTMENT OF THE CHRISTIAN WAY

1 *John* 3: 10–18 (*continued*)

In this passage there is a parenthesis; we return to it now.

The parenthesis is verse 11 and the conclusion drawn from it is in verse 12. The Christian must not be like Cain who murdered his brother.

John goes on to ask why Cain murdered his brother; and his answer is that it was because his works were evil and his brother's were good. Then he drops the remark: "Do not be surprised, brothers, if the world hates you."

An evil man will instinctively hate a good man. Righteousness always provokes hostility in the minds of those whose actions are evil. The reason is that the good man is a walking rebuke to the evil man, even if he never speaks a word to him, his life passes a silent judgment. Socrates was the good man *par excellence*; Alcibiades was brilliant but erratic and often debauched. He used to say to Socrates: "Socrates, I hate you, because every time I meet you you show me what I am."

The *Wisdom of Solomon* has a grim passage (2: 10–20). In it the evil man is made to express his attitude to the good man: "Let us lie in wait for the righteous; because he is not for our turn, and he is clean contrary to our doings. . . . He was made to reprove our thoughts. He is grievous unto us even to behold: for his life is not like other men's, his ways are of another fashion. We are esteemed of him as counterfeits: he abstaineth from our ways as from filthiness." The very sight of the good man made the evil man hate him.

Wherever the Christian is, even though he speak no word, he acts as the conscience of society; and for that very reason the world will often hate him.

In ancient Athens the noble Aristides was unjustly condemned to death; and, when one of the jurymen was asked how he could have cast his vote against such a man, his answer was that he was tired of hearing Aristides called "The Just." The hatred of the world for the Christian is an ever-present phenomenon, and it is due to the fact that the worldly man sees in the Christian the condemnation of himself; he sees in the Christian what he is not and what in his heart of hearts he knows he ought to be; and, because he will not change, he seeks to eliminate the man who reminds him of the lost goodness.

THE ONLY TEST

1 *John* 3: 19–24a

By this we know that we are of the truth, and by this we will reassure our heart before him, when our heart condemns us in

anything, for God is greater than our hearts and knows all things.
Beloved, if our heart does not condemn us, we can come con-
fidently to God and receive from him whatever we ask, because
we keep his commandments and do the things which are well
pleasing to him. And this is his commandment, that we should
believe in the name of his Son Jesus Christ and that we should
love one another, even as he gave us his commandment. And
he who keeps his commandment abides in him and he in him.

INTO the human heart there are bound to come doubts. Any
man with a sensitive mind and heart must sometimes wonder
if he really is a Christian at all. John's test is quite simple
and far-reaching. It is love. If we feel love for our fellow-men
welling up within our hearts, we can be sure that the heart
of Christ is in us. John would have said that a so-called
heretic whose heart was overflowing with love and whose
life was beautiful with service, was far nearer Christ than
someone who was impeccably orthodox, yet cold and remote
from the needs of others.

John goes on to say something which, as far as the Greek
goes, can mean two things. That feeling of love can reassure
us in the presence of God. Our hearts may condemn us
but God is greater than our hearts. The question is: what is the
meaning of this last phrase?

(i) It could mean: since our hearts condemn us and God
is infinitely greater than our hearts, God must condemn us
even more. If we take it that way, it leaves us only with the
fear of God and with nothing to say but: "God be merciful to
me, a sinner." That is a possible translation and no doubt it
is true; but it is not what John is saying in this context,
for here he is thinking of our confidence in God and not
our dread of him.

(ii) The passage must therefore mean this. Our hearts
condemn us—that is inevitable. But God is greater than our
hearts; he knows all things. Not only does he know our
sins; he also knows our love, our longings, the nobility that
never fully works itself out, our penitence; and the greatness

of his knowledge gives him the sympathy which can understand and forgive.

It is this very knowledge of God which gives us our hope. "Man," as Thomas à Kempis said, "sees the deed, but God knows the intention." Men can judge us only by our actions, but God can judge us by the longings which never became deeds and the dreams which never came true. When Solomon was dedicating the Temple, he spoke of how David had wished to build a house for God and how that privilege had been denied to him. "It was in the heart of David, my father, to build a house for the name of the Lord God of Israel. And the Lord said unto David, my father, 'Whereas it was in your heart to build a house for my name, you did well that it was in your heart'" (1 *Kings* 8: 17, 18). The French proverb says, "To know all is to forgive all." God judges us by the deep emotions of the heart; and, if in our heart there is love, then, however feeble and imperfect that love may be, we can with confidence enter into his presence. The perfect knowledge which belongs to God, and to God alone, is not our terror but our hope.

THE INSEPARABLE COMMANDS

1 *John* 3: 19–24a (*continued*)

JOHN goes on to speak of the two things which are well-pleasing in God's sight, the two commandments on obedience to which our relationship to God depends.

(i) We must believe in the name of his Son Jesus Christ. Here we have that use of the word *name* which is peculiar to the biblical writers. It does not mean simply the name by which a person is called; it means the whole nature and character of that person as far as it is known to us. The Psalmist writes: "Our help is in the name of the Lord" (*Psalm* 124: 8). Clearly that does not mean that our help lies in the fact that God is called Jehovah; it means that our help is in the love and mercy and power which have been revealed to us as the nature and character of God. So, then, to believe in the *name* of Jesus Christ, means to believe in the nature and character of Jesus Christ. It means to believe that he is the Son of God, that he does stand in relation to God in a way in which no other person in the universe ever stood or ever can stand, that he can perfectly reveal God to men and that he is the Saviour of our souls. To believe in the name of Jesus Christ is to accept him for what he really is.

(ii) We must love one another, even as he gave us his commandment. This commandment is in *John* 13: 34. We must love each other with that same selfless, sacrificial, forgiving love with which Jesus Christ loved us.

When we put these two commandments together, we find the great truth that the Christian life depends on right belief and right conduct combined. We cannot have the one without the other. There can be no such thing as a Christian theology without a Christian ethic; and equally there can be no such thing as a Christian ethic without a Christian theology. Our belief is not real belief unless it issues in action; and our action has neither sanction nor dynamic unless it is based on belief.

We cannot begin the Christian life until we accept Jesus Christ for what he is; and we have not accepted him in any real sense of the term until our attitude to men is the same as his own attitude of love.

THE PERILS OF THE SURGING LIFE OF THE SPIRIT

1 *John* 3: 24b–4: 1

This is how we know that he abides in us, by the Spirit which he gave to us. Beloved, do not believe every spirit, but test the spirits to see if their source is God, because many false prophets have gone out into the world.

BEHIND this warning is a situation of which we in the modern church know little or nothing. In the early church there was a surging life of the Spirit which brought its own perils. There were so many and such diverse spiritual manifestations that some kind of test was necessary. Let us try to think ourselves back into that electric atmosphere.

(i) Even in Old Testament times men realized the perils of false prophets who were men of spiritual power. *Deuteronomy* 13: 1–5 demands that the false prophet who sought to lure men away from the true God should be put to death; but it frankly and freely admits that he may promise signs and wonders and perform them. The spiritual power is there, but it is evil and misdirected.

(ii) In the early church the spiritual world was very near. All the world believed in a universe thronged with demons and spirits. Every rock and tree and river and grove and lake and mountain had its spiritual power; and these spiritual powers were always seeking entry into men's bodies and minds. In the time of the early church all men lived in a haunted world and men were never so conscious of being surrounded by spiritual powers.

(iii) That ancient world was very conscious of a personal power of evil. It did not speculate about its source, but it was sure that it was there and that it was seeking for men who might be its instruments. It follows that not only the universe but also the minds of men provided the battleground on which the power of the light and the power of the dark fought out the issue.

(iv) In the early church the coming of the Spirit was a much more visible phenomenon than is common nowadays. It was usually connected with baptism; and when the Spirit came things happened that anyone could see. The man who received the Spirit was visibly affected. When the apostles came down to Samaria, after the preaching of Philip, and conferred the gift of the Spirit on the new converts, the effects were so startling that the local magician, Simon Magus, wished to buy the power to produce them (*Acts* 8: 17, 18).

The coming of the Spirit on Cornelius and his people was something which anyone could see (*Acts* 10: 44, 45). In the early church there was an ecstatic element in the coming of the Spirit whose effects were violent and obvious.

(v) This had its effect in the congregational life of the early church. The best commentary on this passage of John is, in fact, 1 *Corinthians* 14. Because of the power of the Spirit men spoke with tongues. That is to say, they poured out a flood of Spirit-given sounds in no known language, which no one could understand unless there was someone present who had the Spirit-given power to interpret. So extraordinary was this phenomenon that Paul does not hesitate to say that, if a stranger came into a congregation in which it was in action, he would think that he had arrived in an assembly of madmen (1 *Corinthians* 14: 2, 23, 27). Even the prophets, who delivered their message in plain language, were a problem. They were so moved by the Spirit that they could not wait for each other to finish and each would leap to his feet determined to shout out his Spirit-given message (1 *Corinthians* 14: 26, 27, 33). A service of worship in an early Christian congregation was very different from the placidity of most modern church services. So diverse were the manifestations of the Spirit that Paul numbers the *discerning of spirits* among the spiritual gifts which a Christian might possess (1 *Corinthians* 12: 10). We can see what might happen in such a case when Paul speaks of the possibility of a man saying in a spirit that Christ is accursed (1 *Corinthians* 12: 3).

When we come further down in Christian history we find the problem still more acute. The *Didache, The Teaching of the Twelve Apostles*, is the first service order book and is to be dated not long after A.D. 100. It has regulations on how to deal with the wandering apostles and prophets who came and went amongst the Christian congregations. "Not every one who speaks in a spirit is a prophet; he is only a prophet if he walks in the ways of the Lord" (*Didache* 11 and 12). The matter reached its peak and *ne plus ultra* when, in the third century, Montanus burst upon the Church with the claim that he was nothing less than the promised Paraclete and that he proposed to tell the Church the things which Christ had said his apostles could not at the moment bear.

The early church was full of this surging life of the Spirit. The exuberance of life had not been organized out of the Church. It was a great age; but its very exuberance had its dangers. If there was a personal power of evil, men could be used by him. If there were evil spirits as well as the Holy Spirit, men could be occupied by them. Men could delude themselves into a quite subjective experience in which they thought—quite honestly—that they had a message from the Spirit.

All this is in John's mind; and it is in face of that surging atmosphere of pulsating spiritual life that he sets out his criteria to judge between the true and the false. We, for our part, may well feel that with all its perils, the exuberant vitality of the early church was a far better thing than the apathetic placidity of so much of the life of the modern church. It was surely better that men should expect the Spirit everywhere than that they should expect him nowhere.

A Note on the Translation of 1 *John* 4: 1–7

There is a recurring Greek phrase in this passage which is by no means easy to translate. It is the phrase which the Revised Standard Version consistently renders *of God*. Its occurrences are as follows:

Verse 1: Test the spirits to see whether they are *of God*.

Verse 2: Every spirit which confesses that Jesus Christ has come in the flesh is *of God*.

Verse 3: Every spirit which does not confess Jesus Christ is not *of God*.

Verse 4: Little children, you are *of God*.

Verse 6: We are *of God*. . . . He who is not *of God* does not listen to us.

Verse 7: Love is *of God*.

The difficulty can be seen in the expedients to which various translators are driven.

Moffatt, in verses 1, 2 and 3, translates *comes from God*; and in verses 4, 6 and 7 *belongs to God*.

Weymouth, in verses 1, 2 and 3, translates *is from God*. In verse 4 he translates: *You are God's children*. In verse 6 he translates: We are *God's children*. . . . He who is not *a child of God* does not listen to us. In verse 7 he has: Love *has its origin in God*.

In every case, except verse 7, Kingsley Williams translates *from God*; in verse 7 he has *of God*.

The difficulty is easy to see; and yet it is of the first importance to be able to attach a precise meaning to this phrase. The Greek is *ek tou theou*. *Ho theos* means *God*, and *tou theou* is the genitive case after the preposition *ek*. *Ek* is one of the commonest Greek prepositions and means *out of* or *from*. To say that a man came *ek tēs poleōs* would mean that he came either *out of* or *from* the city. What then does it mean that a person, or a spirit, or a quality is *ek tou theou*? The simplest translation is *from God*. But what does *from* mean in that phrase? Quite certainly it means that the person, the spirit or the quality *has its origin in God*. It comes from God in the sense that it takes its origin in him and its life from him. So John, for instance, bids his people to test the spirits to see whether they really have their source in God. Love, he says, has its origin in God.

THE ULTIMATE HERESY

1 *John* 4: 2, 3

This is how you recognize the spirit whose source is God. Every spirit which openly acknowledges that Jesus has come in the flesh and is Christ has its origin in God. And every spirit which is such that it does not make this confession about Jesus has not its source in God; and this is the spirit of Antichrist, about which you heard that it was to come and which is now here present in the world.

For John Christian belief could be summed up in one great

sentence: "The Word became flesh and dwelt among us" (*John* 1:14). Any spirit which denied the reality of the Incarnation was not of God. John lays down two tests of belief.

(i) To be of God a spirit must acknowledge that Jesus is the Christ, the Messiah. As John saw it, to deny that is to deny three things about Jesus. (*a*) It is to deny that he is the centre of history, the one for whom all previous history had been a preparation. (*b*) It is to deny that he is the fulfilment of the promises of God. All through their struggles and their defeats, the Jews had clung to the promises of God. To deny that Jesus is the promised Messiah is to deny that these promises were true. (*c*) It is to deny his Kingship. Jesus came, not only to sacrifice, but to reign; and to deny his Messiahship is to leave out his essential kingliness.

(ii) To be of God a spirit must acknowledge that Jesus has come in the flesh. It was precisely this that the Gnostics could never accept. Since, in their view, matter was altogether evil, a real incarnation was an impossibility, for God could never take flesh upon himself. Augustine was later to say that in the pagan philosophers he could find parallels for everything in the New Testament except for one saying—"The Word became flesh." As John saw it, to deny the complete manhood of Jesus Christ was to strike at the very roots of the Christian faith.

To deny the reality of the incarnation has certain definite consequences.

(i) It is to deny that Jesus can ever be our example. If he was not in any real sense a man, living under the same conditions as men, he cannot show men how to live.

(ii) It is to deny that Jesus can be the High Priest who opens the way to God. The true High Priest, as the writer to the Hebrews saw, must be like us in all things, knowing our infirmities and our temptations (*Hebrews* 4:14, 15). To lead men to God the High Priest must be a man, or else he will be pointing them to a road which it is impossible for them to take.

(iii) It is to deny that Jesus can in any real sense be Saviour. To save men he had to identify himself with the men he came to save.

(iv) It is to deny the salvation of the body. Christian teaching is quite clear that salvation is the salvation of the whole man. The body as well as the soul is saved. To deny the incarnation is to deny the possibility that the body can ever become the temple of the Holy Spirit.

(v) By far the most serious and terrible thing is that it is to deny that there can ever be any real union between God and man. If spirit is altogether good and the body is altogether evil, God and man can never meet, so long as man is man. They might meet when man has sloughed off the body and become a *disembodied* spirit. But the great truth of the incarnation is that here and now there can be real communion between God and man.

Nothing in Christianity is more central than the reality of the manhood of Jesus Christ.

THE CLEAVAGE BETWEEN THE WORLD AND GOD

1 *John* 4: 4-6

You have your origin in God, dear children, and you have won the victory over them, because that power which is in you is greater than the power which is in the world. This is why the source of their speaking is the world, and is the reason why the world listens to them. Our source is God. He who knows God listens to us. He who has not his source in God does not listen to us. This is how we know the spirit of truth and the spirit of error.

JOHN lays down a great truth and faces a great problem.

(i) The Christian need not fear the heretic. In Christ the victory over all the powers of evil was won. The powers of evil did their worst to him, even to killing him on a Cross, and in the end he emerged victorious. That victory belongs to the Christian. Whatever things may look like, the powers of evil are fighting a losing battle. As the Latin proverb has it: "Great is the truth, and in the end it will prevail." All that the Christian has to do is remember the truth he already knows and cling to it. The truth is that by which men live; error is ultimately that by which men die.

(ii) The problem remains that the false teachers will neither listen to, nor accept, the truth which the true Christian offers. How is that to be explained? John returns to his favourite antithesis, the opposition between the world and God. The world, as we have seen before, is human nature apart from, and in opposition to, God. The man whose source is God will welcome the truth; the man whose source is the world will reject it.

When we come to think of it, that is an obvious truth. How can a man whose watchword is competition even begin to understand an ethic whose key-note is service? How can a man whose aim is the exaltation of the self and who holds that the weakest must go to the wall, even begin to understand a teaching whose principle for living is love? How can a man who believes that this is the only world and that, therefore, material things are the only ones which matter, even begin to understand life lived in the light of eternity, where the unseen things are the greatest values? A man can hear only what he has fitted himself to hear and he can utterly unfit himself to hear the Christian message.

That is what John is saying. We have seen again and again that it is characteristic of him to see things in terms of black and white. His thinking does not deal in shades. On the one side there is the man whose source and origin is God and who can hear the truth; on the other side there is the man whose source and origin is the world and who is incapable of hearing the truth. There emerges a problem, which very likely John did not even think of. Are there people to whom all preaching is quite useless? Are there people whose defences can never be penetrated, whose deafness can never hear, and whose minds are for ever shut to the invitation and command of Jesus Christ?

The answer must be that there are no limits to the grace of God and that there is such a person as the Holy Spirit. It is the lesson of life that the love of God can break every barrier down. It is true that a man can resist; it is, maybe, true that a man can resist even to the end. But what is also true is that Christ is always knocking at the door of every heart, and it is possible for any man to hear the voice of Christ, even above the many voices of the world.

LOVE HUMAN AND DIVINE

1 *John* 4: 7–21

Beloved, let us love one another, because love has its source in God, and everyone who loves has God as the source of his birth and knows God. He who does not love has not come to know God. In this God's love is displayed within us, that God sent his only Son into the world that through him we might live. In this is love, not that we love God, but that he loved us and sent his Son to be an atoning sacrifice for our sins. Brothers, if God so loved us, we too ought to love each other. No one has ever seen God. If we love each other God dwells in us and his love is perfected in us. It is by this that we know that we dwell in him and he in us, because he has given us a share of his Spirit. We have seen and we testify that the Father sent the Son as the Saviour of the world. Whoever openly acknowledges that Jesus is the Son of God, God dwells in him and he in God. We have come to know and to put our trust in the love which God has within us. God is love and he who dwells in love dwells in God and God dwells in him. With us love finds its peak in this, that we should have confidence in the day of judgment because, even as he is, so also are we in this world. There is no fear in love; but perfect love casts out fear, for fear is connected with punishment and he who fears has not reached love's perfect state. We love because he first loved us. If any one says, "I love God" and hates his brother, he is a liar; for he who does not love his brother, whom he has seen, cannot love God whom he has not seen. It is this command that we have from him, that he who loves God, loves his brother also.

THIS passage is so closely interwoven that we are better to read it as a whole and then bit by bit to draw out its teaching. First of all, then, let us look at its teaching on love.

(i) Love has its origin in God (verse 7). It is from the God who is love that all love takes its source. As A. E. Brooke puts it: "Human love is a reflection of something in the divine nature itself." We are never nearer to God than when we love. Clement of Alexandria said in a startling phrase that the real Christian "practises being God." He who dwells in love dwells in God (verse 16). Man is made in the image and the likeness of God (*Genesis* 1: 26). God is love and, therefore, to be like God and be what he was meant to be, man must also love.

(ii) Love has a double relationship to God. It is only by knowing God that we learn to love and it is only by loving that we learn to know God (verses 7 and 8). Love comes from God, and love leads to God.

(iii) It is by love that God is known (verse 12). We cannot see God, because he is spirit; what we can see is his effect. We cannot see the wind, but we can see what it can do. We cannot see electricity, but we can see the effect it produces. The effect of God is love. It is when God comes into a man that he is clothed with the love of God and the love of men. God is known by his effect on that man. It has been said, "A saint is a man in whom Christ lives again" and the best demonstration of God comes not from argument but from a life of love.

(iv) God's love is demonstrated in Jesus Christ (verse 9). When we look at Jesus we see two things about the love of God. (*a*) It is a love which holds nothing back. God was prepared to give his only Son and make a sacrifice beyond which no sacrifice can possibly go in his love for men. (*b*) It is a totally undeserved love. It would be no wonder if we loved God, when we remember all the gifts he has given to us, even apart from Jesus Christ; the wonder is that he loves poor and disobedient creatures like us.

> How thou canst think so well of us,
>   And be the God thou art,
> Is darkness to my intellect,
>   But sunshine to my heart.

(v) Human love is a response to divine love (verse 19). We love because God loved us. It is the sight of his love which wakens in us the desire to love him as he first loved us and to love our fellow-men as he loves them.

(vi) When love comes, fear goes (verses 17 and 18). Fear is the characteristic emotion of someone who expects to be punished. So long as we regard God as the Judge, the King, the Law-giver, there can be nothing in our heart but fear for in face of such a God we can expect nothing but punishment. But once we know God's true nature, fear is swallowed up in love. The fear that remains is the fear of grieving his love for us.

(vii) Love of God and love of man are indissolubly connected (verses 7, 11, 20, 21). As C. H. Dodd finely puts it: "The energy of love discharges itself along lines which form a triangle, whose points are God, self, and neighbour." If God loves us, we are bound to love each other, because it is our destiny to reproduce the life of God in humanity and the life of eternity in time. John says, with almost crude bluntness, that a man who claims to love God and hates his brother is nothing other than a liar. The only way to prove that we love God is to love the men whom God loves. The only way to prove that God is within our hearts is constantly to show the love of men within our lives.

GOD IS LOVE

1 *John* 4: 7–21 (*continued*)

IN this passage there occurs what is probably the greatest single statement about God in the whole Bible, that *God is love*. It is amazing how many doors that single statement unlocks and how many questions it answers.

(i) It is the explanation of *creation*. Sometimes we are bound to wonder why God created this world. The disobedience, and the lack of response in men is a continual grief to him. Why should he create a world which was to bring him nothing but trouble? The answer is that creation was essential to his very nature. If God is love, he cannot exist in lonely isolation. Love must have someone to love and someone to love it.

(ii) It is the explanation of *free-will*. Unless love is a free response it is not love. Had God been only law he could have created a world in which men moved like automata, having no more choice than a machine. But, if God had made men like that, there would have been no possibility of a personal relationship between him and them. Love is of necessity the free response of the heart; and, therefore, God, by a deliberate act of self-limitation, had to endow men with free will.

(iii) It is the explanation of *providence*. Had God been simply mind and order and law, he might, so to speak, have created the universe, wound it up, set it going and left it. There are articles and machines which we are urged to buy because we can fit them and forget them; their most attractive quality is that they can be left to run themselves. But, because God is love, his creating act is followed by his constant care.

(iv) It is the explanation of *redemption*. If God had been only law and justice, he would simply have left men to the consequences of their sin. The moral law would operate; the soul that sinned would die; and the eternal justice would inexorably hand out its punishments. But the very fact that God is love meant that he had to seek and save that which was lost. He had to find a remedy for sin.

(v) It is the explanation of the *life beyond*. If God were simply creator, men might live their brief span and die for ever. The life which ended early would be only another flower which the frost of death had withered too soon. But the fact that God is love makes it certain that the chances and changes

of life have not the last word and that his love will readjust
the balance of this life.

SON OF GOD AND SAVIOUR OF MEN

1 *John* 4: 7–21 (*continued*)

BEFORE we leave this passage we must note that it has also
great things to say about Jesus Christ.

(i) It tells us that Jesus is *the bringer of life*. God sent him
that through him we might have life (verse 9). There is a
world of difference between existence and life. All men have
existence but all do not have life. The very eagerness with
which men seek pleasure shows that there is something missing
in their lives. A famous doctor once said that men would
find a cure for cancer more quickly than they would find
a cure for boredom. Jesus gives a man an object for which to
live; he gives him strength by which to live; and he gives him
peace in which to live. Living with Christ turns mere
existence into fullness of life.

(ii) It tells us that Jesus is *the restorer of the lost relationship
with God*. God sent him to be the atoning sacrifice for sin
(verse 10). We do not move in a world of thought in which
animal sacrifice is a reality. But we can fully understand
what sacrifice meant. When a man sinned, his relationship
with God was broken; and sacrifice was an expression of
penitence, designed to restore the lost relationship. Jesus, by
his life and death, made it possible for man to enter into a
new relationship of peace and friendship with God. He bridged
the awful gulf between man and God.

(iii) It tells us that Jesus is *the Saviour of the world* (verse
14). When he came into the world, men were conscious of
nothing so much as their own weakness and helplessness.
Men, said Seneca, were looking *ad salutem*, for salvation.
They were desperately conscious of "their weakness in
necessary things." They wanted "a hand let down to lift them

up." It would be quite inadequate to think of salvation as mere deliverance from the punishment of hell. Men need to be saved from themselves; they need to be saved from the habits which have become their fetters; they need to be saved from their temptations; they need to be saved from their fears and their anxieties; they need to be saved from their follies and mistakes. In every case Jesus offers men salvation; he brings that which enables them to face time and to meet eternity.

(iv) It tells us that Jesus is *the Son of God* (verse 15). Whatever that may mean, it certainly means that Jesus Christ is in a relationship to God in which no other person ever stood or ever will stand. He alone can show men what God is like; he alone can bring to men God's grace, love, forgiveness and strength.

One other thing emerges in this passage. It has taught us of God and it has taught us of Jesus; and it teaches us of the Spirit. In verse 13 John says it is because we have a share of the Spirit that we know that we dwell in God. It is the work of the Spirit that in the beginning makes us seek God at all; it is the work of the Spirit that makes us aware of God's presence; and it is the work of the Spirit that gives us the certainty that we are truly at peace with God. It is the Spirit in our hearts which makes us dare to address God as Father (*Romans* 8: 15, 16). The Spirit is the inner witness who, as C. H. Dodd puts it, gives us the "immediate, spontaneous, unanalysable awareness of a divine presence in our lives."

> "And his that gentle voice we hear,
>   Soft as the breath of even,
> That checks each fault, that calms each fear,
>   And speaks of heaven.
>
> And every virtue we possess,
>   And every victory won,
> And every thought of holiness,
>   Are his alone."

LOVE WITHIN THE DIVINE FAMILY

1 *John* 5: 1, 2

> Everyone who believes that Jesus is the Christ has experienced
> the birth which comes from God; and everyone who loves the father
> loves the child. This is how we know that we must be loving the
> children of God, whenever we love God and keep his com-
> mandments.

As John wrote this passage, there were two things in the
background of his mind.

(i) There was the great fact which was the basis of all
his thinking, the fact that love of God and love of man are
inseparable parts of the same experience. In answer to the
questioning scribe Jesus had said that there were two great
commandments. The first laid it down that we must love God
with all our heart and soul and mind and strength; and the
second laid it down that we must love our neighbour as
ourselves. Than these commandments there are none greater
(*Mark* 12: 28–31). John had in mind this word of his Lord.

(ii) But he also had in mind a natural law of human life.
Family love is a part of nature. The child naturally loves his
parents; and he just as naturally loves his brothers and sisters.
The second part of verse 1 literally runs: "Everyone who loves
him who begat, loves him who was begotten of him." Put
much more simply that is: "If we love a father, we also love
his child." John is thinking of the love which naturally binds
a man to the father who begat him and to the other children
whom the father has begotten.

John transfers this to the realm of Christian thought and
experience. The Christian undergoes the experience of being
reborn; the father is God; and the Christian is bound to
love God for all that he has done for his soul. But birth is
always into a family; and the Christian is reborn into the
family of God. As it was for Jesus, so it is for him—those
who do the will of God, as he himself does, become his
mother, his sisters and his brothers (*Mark* 3: 35). If, then, the
Christian loves God the Father who begat him, he must also

love the other children whom God has begotten. His love of God and his love of his Christian brothers and sisters must be parts of the same love, so closely interlocked that they can never be separated.

It has been put: "Man is not only born *to love*, he is also born *to be loved*." A. E. Brooke put it: "Everyone who has been born of God must love those who have been similarly ennobled."

Long before this the Psalmist had said that, "God gives the desolate a home to dwell in" (*Psalm* 68: 6). The Christian by virtue of his rebirth is set within the family of God and as he loves the Father, so must he also love the children who are of the same family as he is.

THE NECESSARY OBEDIENCE

1 *John* 5: 3, 4a

For this is the love of God, that we should keep his commandments; and his commandments are not heavy, because everything that is born of God conquers the world.

JOHN reverts to an idea which is never far from the surface of his mind. *Obedience is the only proof of love*. We cannot prove our love to anyone other than by seeking to please him and bring him joy.

Then John quite suddenly says a most surprising thing. God's commandments, he says, are not heavy. We must note two general things here.

He certainly does not mean that obedience to God's commandments is easy to achieve. Christian love is no easy matter. It is never an easy thing to love people whom we do not like or people who hurt our feelings or injure us. It is never an easy thing to solve the problem of living together; and when it becomes the problem of living together on the Christian standard of life, it is a task of immense difficulty.

Further, there is in this saying an implied contrast. Jesus

spoke of the Scribes and Pharisees as "binding heavy burdens
and hard to bear, and laying them on men's shoulders"
(*Matthew* 23: 4). The Scribal and Pharisaic mass of rules and
regulations could be an intolerable burden on the shoulders
of any man. There is no doubt that John is remembering
that Jesus said, "My yoke is easy and my burden is light"
(*Matthew* 11: 30).

How then is this to be explained? How can it be said
that the tremendous demands of Jesus are not a heavy burden?
There are three answers to that question.

(i) It is the way of God never to lay a commandment on
any man without also giving him the strength to carry it out.
With the vision comes the power; with the need for it comes
the strength. God does not give us his commandments and
then go away and leave us to ourselves. He is there by our
side to enable us to carry out what he has commanded. What
is impossible for us becomes possible with God.

(ii) But there is another great truth here. Our response to
God must be the response of love; and for love no duty
is too hard and no task too great. That which we would
never do for a stranger we will willingly attempt for a loved
one. What would be an impossible sacrifice, if a stranger
demanded it, becomes a willing gift when love needs it.

There is an old story which is a kind of parable of this.
Someone once met a lad going to school long before the days
when transport was provided. The lad was carrying on his back
a smaller boy who was clearly lame and unable to walk. The
stranger said to the lad, "Do you carry him to school every
day?" "Yes," said the boy. "That's a heavy burden for you
to carry," said the stranger. "He's no' a burden," said the
boy. "He's my brother."

Love turned the burden into no burden at all. It must be so
with us and Christ. His commandments are not a burden
but a privilege and an opportunity to show our love.

Difficult the commandments of Christ are, burdensome they
are not; for Christ never laid a commandment on a man
without giving him the strength to carry it; and every com-

mandment laid upon us provides another chance to show our love.

We must leave the third answer to our next section.

THE CONQUEST OF THE WORLD

1 *John* 5: 4b, 5

> And this is the conquest which has conquered the world, our faith. Who is he who conquers the world but he who believes that Jesus is the Son of God?

(iii) We have seen that the commandments of Jesus Christ are not grievous because with the commandment there comes the power and because we accept them in love. But there is another great truth. There is something in the Christian which makes him able to conquer the world. The *kosmos* is the world apart from God and in opposition to him. That which enables us to conquer the *kosmos* is *faith*.

John defines this conquering faith as the belief that Jesus is the Son of God. It is belief in the Incarnation. Why should that be so victory-giving? If we believe in the incarnation, it means that we believe that in Jesus God entered the world and took our human life upon himself. If he did that, it means that he *cared* enough for men to take upon himself the limitations of humanity, which is the act of a love that passes human understanding. If God did that, it means that he *shares* in all the manifold activities of human life and knows the many and varied trials and temptations and sorrows of this world. It means that everything that happens to us is fully understood by God and that he is in this business of living along with us. Faith in the incarnation is the conviction that God shares and God cares. Once we possess that faith certain things follow.

(i) We have a defence to resist the infections of the world. On all sides there is the pressure of worldly standards and motives; on all sides the fascinations of the wrong things.

From within and without come the temptations which are part of the human situation in a world and a society not interested in and sometimes hostile to God. But once we are aware of the presence of God in Jesus Christ ever with us, we have a strong prophylactic against the infections of the world. It is a fact of experience that goodness is easier in the company of good people; and if we believe in the incarnation, we have the continual presence of God in Jesus Christ.

(ii) We have a strength to endure the attacks of the world. The human situation is full of things which seek to take our faith away. There are the sorrows and the perplexities of life; there are the disappointments and the frustrations of life; there are for most of us the failures and discouragements of life. But if we believe in the incarnation, we believe in a God who himself went through all this, even to the Cross and who can, therefore, help others who are going through it.

(iii) We have the indestructible hope of final victory. The world did its worst to Jesus. It hounded him and slandered him. It branded him heretic and friend of sinners. It judged him and crucified him and buried him. It did everything humanly possible to eliminate him—*and it failed*. After the Cross came the Resurrection; after the shame came the glory. That is the Jesus who is with us, one who saw life at its grimmest, to whom life did its worst, who died, who conquered death, and who offers us a share in that victory which was his. If we believe that Jesus is the Son of God, we have with us always Christ the Victor to make us victorious.

THE WATER AND THE BLOOD

1 *John* 5: 6–8

This is he who came through water and blood—Jesus Christ. It was not only by water that he came, but by water and by blood. And it is the Spirit which testifies to this, because the Spirit is truth; because there are three who testify, the Spirit and the water and the blood, and the three agree in one.

PLUMMER, in beginning to comment on this passage says: "This is the most perplexing passage in the Epistle, and one of the most perplexing in the New Testament." No doubt, if we knew the circumstances in which John was writing and had full knowledge of the heresies against which he was defending his people, the meaning would become clear but, as it is, we can only guess. We do, however, know enough of the background to be fairly sure that we can come at the meaning of John's words.

It is clear that the words *water* and *blood* in connection with Jesus had for John a special mystical and symbolic meaning. In his story of the Cross there is a curious pair of verses:

> One of the soldiers pierced his side with a spear, and at once there came out blood and water. He who saw it has borne witness— his testimony is true, and he knows that he tells the truth—that you also may believe (*John* 19: 34, 35).

Clearly John attaches particular importance to that incident and he guarantees it with a very special certificate of evidence. To him the words *water* and *blood* in connection with Jesus conveyed an essential part of the meaning of the gospel.

The first verse of the passage is obscurely expressed—"This is he who came through water and blood—Jesus Christ." The meaning is that this is he who entered into his Messiahship or was shown to be the Christ through water and blood.

In connection with Jesus *water* and *blood* can refer only to two events of his life. The *water* must refer to his *baptism*; the *blood* to his *Cross*. John is saying that *both* the baptism and the Cross of Jesus are essential parts of his Messiahship. He goes on to say that it was not by water only that he came, but by water *and* by blood. It is, then, clear that some were saying that Jesus came by water, but not by blood; in other words that his baptism was an essential part of his Messiahship but his Cross was not. This is what gives us our clue to what lies behind this passage.

We have seen again and again that behind this letter lies

the heresy of Gnosticism. And we have also seen that
Gnosticism, believing that Spirit was altogether good and
matter altogether evil, denied that God came in the flesh.
So they had a belief of which Irenaeus tells us connected with
the name of Cerinthus, one of their principal representatives
and an exact contemporary of John. Cerinthus taught that
at the baptism the divine Christ descended into the man
Jesus in the form of a dove; Jesus, allied as it were with the
Christ who had descended upon him, brought to men the
message of the God who had hitherto been unknown and
lived in perfect virtue; then the Christ departed from the man
Jesus and returned to glory, and it was only the man Jesus
who was crucified on Calvary and afterwards resurrected. We
might put it more simply by saying that Cerinthus taught
that Jesus became divine at the baptism, that divinity left
him before the Cross and that he died simply a man.

It is clear that such teaching robs the life and death of
Jesus of all value for us. By seeking to protect God from
contact with human pain, it removes him from the act of
redemption.

What John is saying is that the Cross is an essential part
of the meaning of Jesus and that God was in the death of
Jesus every bit as much as he was in his life.

THE TRIPLE WITNESS

1 *John* 5: 6–8 (*continued*)

JOHN goes on to speak of the triple witness.

There is the witness of *the Spirit*. In this John is thinking
of three things. (i) The New Testament story is clear that
at his baptism the Spirit descended upon Jesus in the most
special way (*Mark* 1: 9–11; *Matthew* 3: 16, 17; *Luke* 3: 21,
22; *Acts* 10: 38; *John* 1: 32–34). (ii) The New Testament is
also clear that, while John came to baptize with water, Jesus
came to baptize with the Spirit (*Mark* 1: 8; *Matthew* 3: 11;

Luke 3: 16; *Acts* 1: 5; 2: 33). He came to bring men the Spirit with a plentitude and a power hitherto quite unknown. (iii) The history of the early church is the proof that this was no idle claim. It began at Pentecost (*Acts* 2: 4), and it repeated itself over and over again in the history and experience of the Church (*Acts* 8: 17; 10: 44). Jesus had the Spirit and he could give the Spirit to men; and the continuing evidence of the Spirit in the Church was—and is— an undeniable witness to the continuing power of Jesus Christ.

There is the witness of *the water*. At Jesus's own baptism there was the witness of the Spirit descending upon him. It was, in fact, that event which revealed to John the Baptist who Jesus was. It is John's point that in the early church that witness was maintained in Christian baptism. We must remember that thus early in the Church's history baptism was adult baptism, the confession of faith and the reception into the Church of men and women coming direct from heathenism and beginning an absolutely new way of life. In Christian baptism things happened. A man plunged below the water and died with Christ; he emerged and was resurrected with Christ to a new life. Therefore, Christian baptism was a witness to the continuing power of Jesus Christ. It was a witness that he was still alive and that he was indeed divine.

There was the witness of *the blood*. The blood was the life. In any sacrifice the blood was sacred to God and to God alone. The death of Christ was the perfect sacrifice; in the Cross his blood was poured out to God. It was the experience of men that that sacrifice was availing, that it did redeem them and reconcile them to God and give them peace with God. Continuously in the Church the Lord's Supper, the Eucharist, was and is observed. In it the sacrifice of Christ is full displayed; and in it there is given to men the opportunity not only to give thanks to Christ for his sacrifice made once for all, but also to appropriate its benefits and to avail themselves of its healing power. That happened in John's time. At the Lord's Table men met the Christ and experienced his forgiveness and the peace with God which he brings. Men still have that experience; and, therefore that feast is a continuing witness to the atoning power of the sacrifice of Jesus Christ.

The Spirit and the water and the blood all combine to demonstrate the perfect Messiahship, the perfect Sonship, the perfect Saviourhood of this man Jesus in whom was God. The continued gift of the Spirit, the continued death and resurrection of baptism, the continued availability of the sacrifice of the Cross at the Lord's Table are still the witnesses to Jesus Christ.

Note on 1 *John* 5: 7

In the Authorized Version there is a verse which we have altogether omitted. It reads, "For there are three that bear record in heaven, the Father, the Word and the Holy Ghost; and these three are one."

The Revised Version omits this verse, and does not even mention it in the margin, and none of the newer translations includes it. It is quite certain that it does not belong to the original text.

The facts are as follows. First, it does not occur in any Greek manuscript earlier than the 14th century. The great manuscripts belong to the 3rd and 4th centuries, and it occurs in none of them. None of the great early fathers of the Church knew it. Jerome's original version of the Vulgate does not include it. The first person to quote it is a Spanish heretic called Priscillian who died in A.D. 385. Thereafter it crept gradually into the Latin texts of the New Testament although, as we have seen, it did not gain an entry to the Greek manuscripts.

How then did it get into the text? Originally it must have been a scribal gloss or comment in the margin. Since it seemed to offer good scriptural evidence for the doctrine of the Trinity, through time it came to be accepted by theologians as part of the text, especially in those early days of scholarship before the great manuscripts were discovered.

But how did it last, and how did it come to be in the

Authorized Version? The first Greek testament to be published was that of Erasmus in 1516. Erasmus was a great scholar and, knowing that this verse was not in the original text, he did not include it in his first edition. By this time, however, theologians were using the verse. It had, for instance, been printed in the Latin Vulgate of 1514. Erasmus was therefore criticized for omitting it. His answer was that if anyone could show him a Greek manuscript which had the words in it, he would print them in his next edition. Someone did produce a very late and very bad text in which the verse did occur in Greek; and Erasmus, true to his word but very much against his judgment and his will, printed the verse in his 1522 edition.

The next step was that in 1550 Stephanus printed his great edition of the Greek New Testament. This 1550 edition of Stephanus was called—he gave it that name himself—The Received Text, and it was the basis of the Authorized Version and of the Greek text for centuries to come. That is how this verse got into the Authorized Version. There is, of course, nothing wrong with it; but modern scholarship has made it quite certain that John did not write it and that it is a much later commentary on, and addition to, his words; and that is why all modern translations omit it.

THE UNDENIABLE WITNESS

1 *John* 5: 9, 10

> If we accept the testimony of men, the testimony of God is greater, for this is the testimony of God that he has borne testimony about his Son. He who believes in the Son of God has that testimony within himself. He who does not believe God has made God a liar, because he has not believed in the testimony which God bore to his Son.

BEHIND this passage there are two basic ideas.

There is the Old Testament idea of what constitutes an adequate witness. The law was quite clear: "A single witness shall not prevail against a man for any crime or for any wrong in connection with any offence that he has committed; only on the evidence of two witnesses, or of three witnesses, shall a charge be sustained" (*Deuteronomy* 19: 15; cp. 17: 6). A triple human witness is enough to establish any fact. How much more must a triple divine witness, the witness of the Spirit, the water, and the blood, be regarded as convincing.

Second, the idea of witness is an integral part of John's thought. In his gospel we find different witnesses all converging on Jesus Christ. John the Baptist is a witness to Jesus (*John* 1: 15; 1: 32–34; 5: 33). Jesus's deeds are a witness to, him (*John* 5: 36). The Scriptures are a witness to him (*John* 5: 39). The Father who sent him is a witness to him (*John* 5: 30–32, 37; 8: 18). The Spirit is a witness to him. "When the Counsellor comes . . . even the Spirit of truth . . . he will bear witness to me" (*John* 15: 26).

John goes on to use a phrase which is a favourite of his in his gospel. He speaks of the man who "believes in the Son of God." There is a wide difference between *believing* a man and *believing in* him. If we *believe* a man, we do no more than accept whatever statement he may be making at the moment as true. If we *believe in* a man, we accept the whole man and all that he stands for in complete trust. We would be prepared not only to trust his spoken word, but also to trust ourselves to him. To believe in Jesus Christ is not simply to accept what he says as true; it is to commit ourselves into his hands, for time and for eternity.

When a man does that, the Holy Spirit within him testifies that he is acting aright. It is the Holy Spirit who gives him the conviction of the ultimate value of Jesus Christ and assures him that he is right to make this act of commitment to him. The man who refuses to do that is refusing the promptings of the Holy Spirit within his heart.

If a man refuses to accept the evidence of men who have experienced what Christ can do, the evidence of the deeds of Christ, the evidence of the Scriptures, the evidence of God's Holy Spirit, the evidence of God himself, in effect he is calling God a liar—and that is the very limit of blasphemy.

THE ESSENCE OF THE FAITH

1 *John* 5: 11–13

And this is the testimony, that God gave us eternal life and that that life is in his Son. He who has the Son has life; he who has not the Son has not life. I have written these things to you who believe in the name of the Son of God that you may know that you have eternal life.

WITH this paragraph the letter proper comes to an end. What follows is in the nature of a postscript. The end is a statement that the essence of the Christian life is *eternal life*.

The word for eternal is *aiōnios*. It means far more than simply *lasting for ever*. A life which lasted for ever might well be a curse and not a blessing, an intolerable burden and not a shining gift. There is only one person to whom *aiōnios* may properly be applied and that is God. In the real sense of the term it is God alone who possesses and inhabits eternity. *Eternal life* is, therefore, nothing other than *the life of God himself*. What we are promised is that here and now there can be given us a share in the very life of God.

In God there is *peace* and, therefore, *eternal life* means *serenity*. It means a life liberated from the fears which haunt the human situation. In God there is *power* and, therefore, *eternal life* means *the defeat of frustration*. It means a life filled with the power of God and, therefore, victorious over circumstance. In God there is *holiness* and, therefore, *eternal life* means *the defeat of sin*. It means a life clad with the purity of God and armed against the soiling infections of the world. In God there is *love* and, therefore, *eternal life* means *the end of bitterness and hatred*. It means a life which has the love of God in its heart and the undefeatable love of man in all its feelings and in all its action. In God there is *life* and, therefore *eternal life* means *the defeat of death*. It means a life which is indestructible because it has in it the indestructibility of God himself.

It is John's conviction that such a life comes through Jesus

Christ and in no other way. Why should that be? If eternal life is the life of God, it means that we can possess that life only when we know God and are enabled to approach him and rest in him. We can do these two things only in Jesus Christ. The Son alone fully knows the Father and, therefore, only he can fully reveal to us what God is like. As John had it in his gospel: "No one has ever seen God; the only Son, who is in the bosom of the Father, he has made him known" (*John* 1: 18). And Jesus Christ alone can bring us to God. It is in him that there is open to us the new and living way into the presence of God (*Hebrews* 10: 19–23). We may take a simple analogy. If we wish to meet someone whom we do not know and who moves in a completely different circle from our own, we can achieve that meeting only by finding someone who knows him and is willing to introduce us to him. That is what Jesus does for us in regard to God. Eternal life is the life of God and we can find that life only through Jesus Christ.

THE BASIS AND THE PRINCIPLE OF PRAYER

1 *John* 5: 14, 15

> And this is the confidence that we have towards him, that, if we ask anything which is in accordance with his will, he hears us; and, if we know that he hears anything that we ask, we know that we possess the requests that we have made from him.

HERE are set down both the basis and the principle of prayer.

(i) The *basis of prayer* is the simple fact that God listens to our prayers. The word which John uses for *confidence* is interesting. It is *parrēsia*. Originally *parrēsia* meant *freedom of speech*, that freedom to speak boldly which exists in a true democracy. Later it came to denote any kind of confidence. With God we have freedom of speech. He is always listening, more ready to hear than we are to pray. We never need to force our way into his presence or compel him to pay attention.

He is waiting for us to come. We know how we often wait
for the knock of the postman or the ring of the telephone
bell to bring us a message from someone whom we love. In
all reverence we can say that God is like that with us.

(ii) The *principle* of prayer is that to be answered it must
be *in accordance with the will of God*. Three times in his
writings John lays down what might be called the conditions
of prayer. (*a*) He says that *obedience* is a condition of prayer.
We receive whatever we ask because we keep his commandments (1 *John* 3: 22). (*b*) He says that *remaining in Christ* is
a condition of prayer. If we abide in him and his words
abide in us, we will ask what we will and it will be done
for us (*John* 15: 7). The closer we live to Christ, the more
we shall pray aright; and the more we pray aright, the greater
the answer we receive. (*c*) He says that to pray *in his name*
is a condition of prayer. If we ask anything in his name, he
will do it (*John* 14: 14). The ultimate test of any request is,
can we say to Jesus, "Give me this for *your* sake and in
your name"?

Prayer must be *in accordance with the will of God*. Jesus
teaches us to pray: "Thy will be done," not, "Thy will be
changed." Jesus himself, in the moment of his greatest agony
and crisis, prayed, "Not as I will, but as thou wilt. . . . Thy
will be done" (*Matthew* 26: 39, 42). Here is the very essence
of prayer. C. H. Dodd writes: "Prayer rightly considered is
not a device for employing the resources of omnipotence to
fulfil our own desires, but a means by which our desires may
be redirected according to the mind of God, and made into
channels for the forces of his will." A. E. Brooke suggests
that John thought of prayer as "including only requests for
knowledge of, and acquiescence in, the will of God." Even
the great pagans saw this. Epictetus wrote: "Have courage
to look up to God and say, Deal with me as thou wilt
from now on. I am as one with thee; I am thine; I flinch
from nothing so long as thou dost think that it is good. Lead
me where thou wilt; put on me what raiment thou wilt.
Wouldst thou have me hold office or eschew it, stay or

flee, be rich or poor? For all this I will defend thee before men."

Here is something on which to ponder. We are so apt to think that prayer is asking God for what we want, whereas true prayer is asking God for what he wants. Prayer is not only talking to God, even more it is listening to him.

PRAYING FOR THE BROTHER WHO SINS

1 *John* 5: 16, 17

> If anyone sees his brother sinning a sin which is not a sin whose end is death, he will ask life for him and he will give it to him, that is, to those whose sin is not a sin whose end is death. There is a sin whose end is death. It is not about that that I mean he should ask. All wrongdoing is sin; but there is a sin whose end is not death.

THERE is no doubt that this is a most difficult and disturbing passage. Before we approach its problems, let us look at its certainties.

John has just been speaking about the Christian privilege of prayer; and now he goes on to single out for special attention the prayer of intercession for the brother who needs praying for. It is very significant that, when John speaks about one kind of prayer, it is not prayer for ourselves; it is prayer for others. Prayer must never be selfish; it must never be concentrated entirely upon our own selves and our own problems and our own needs. It must be an outgoing activity. As Westcott put it: "The end of prayer is the perfection of the whole Christian body."

Again and again the New Testament writers stress the need for this prayer of intercession. Paul writes to the Thessalonians: "Brothers, pray for us" (1 *Thessalonians* 5: 25). The writer to the Hebrews says: "Pray for us" (*Hebrews* 13: 18, 19). James says that, if a man is sick, he ought to call the elders, and the elders should pray over him (*James* 5: 14).

It is the advice to Timothy that prayer must be made for all men (1 *Timothy* 2: 1). The Christian has the tremendous privilege of bearing his brother man to the throne of grace. There are three things to be said about this.

(i) We naturally pray for those who are ill, and we should just as naturally pray for those who are straying away from God. It should be just as natural to pray for the cure of the soul as it is to pray for the cure of the body. It may be that there is nothing greater that we can do for the man who is straying away and who is in peril of making shipwreck of his life than to commit him to the grace of God.

(ii) But it must be remembered that, when we have prayed for such a man, our task is not yet done. In this, as in all other things, our first responsibility is to seek to make our own prayers come true. It will often be our duty to speak to the man himself. We must not only speak to God about him, we must also speak to the man about himself. God needs a channel through which his grace can come and an agent through whom he can act; and it may well be that we are to be his voice in this instance.

(iii) We have previously thought about the basis of prayer and about the principle of prayer; but here we meet the limitation of prayer. It may well be that God wishes to answer our prayer; it may well be that we pray with heartfelt sincerity; but God's aim and our prayer can be frustrated by the man for whom we pray. If we pray for a sick person and he disobeys his doctors and acts foolishly, our prayer will be frustrated. God may urge, God may plead, God may warn, God may offer, but not even God can violate the freedom of choice which he himself has given to us. It is often the folly of man which frustrates our prayers and cancels the grace of God.

SIN WHOSE END IS DEATH

1 *John* 5: 16, 17 (*continued*)

THIS passage speaks of the sin whose end is death and the

sin whose end is not death. The Revised Standard Version translates "mortal" sin.

There have been many suggestions in regard to this.

The Jews distinguished two kinds of sins. There were the sins which a man committed unwittingly or, at least, not deliberately. These were sins which a man might commit in ignorance, or when he was swept away by some over-mastering impulse, or in some moment of strong emotion when his passions were too strong for the leash of the will to hold. On the other hand, there were the sins of the high hand and the haughty heart, the sins which a man deliberately committed, the sins in which he defiantly took his own way in spite of the known will of God for him. It was for the first kind of sin that sacrifice atoned; but for the sins of the haughty heart and the high hand no sacrifice could atone.

Plummer lists three suggestions. (i) Mortal sins may be sins which are *punishable* by death. But it is quite clear that more is meant than that. This passage is not thinking of sins which are a breach of man-made laws, however serious. (ii) Mortal sins may be sins which God visits with death. Paul writes to the Corinthians that, because of their unworthy conduct at the table of the Lord, many among them are weak and many are asleep, that is, many have died (1 *Corinthians* 11: 30); and the suggestion is that the reference is to sins which are so serious that God sends death. (iii) Mortal sins may be sins punishable with excommunication from the Church. When Paul is writing to the Corinthians about the notorious sinner with whom they have not adequately dealt, he demands that he should be "delivered to Satan." That was the phrase for excommunication. But he goes on to say that, serious as this punishment is and sore as its bodily consequence may be, it is designed to save the man's soul in the Day of the Lord Jesus (1 *Corinthians* 5: 5). It is a punishment which does not end in death. None of these explanations will do.

There are three further suggestions as to the identification of this mortal sin.

(*a*) There is a line of thought in the New Testament which points to the fact that some held that there was no forgiveness for post-baptismal sin. There were those who believed that baptism cleansed from all previous sins but that after baptism there was no forgiveness. There is an echo of that line of thought in *Hebrews*: "It is impossible to restore again to repentance, those who have once been enlightened, who have tasted the heavenly gift, and have become partakers of the Holy Spirit, and have tasted the goodness of the word of God and the powers of the age to come, if they then commit apostasy" (*Hebrews* 6: 4–6). In early Christian terminology *to be enlightened* was often a technical term for *to be baptized*. It was indeed that belief which made many postpone baptism until the last possible moment. But the real essence of that statement in *Hebrews* is that restoration becomes impossible when penitence has become impossible; the connection is not so much with baptism as with penitence.

(*b*) Later on in the early church there was a strong line of thought which declared that apostasy could never be forgiven. In the days of the great persecutions some said that those who in fear or in torture had denied their faith could never have forgiveness; for had not Jesus said, "Whoever denies me before men, I also will deny before my Father who is in heaven" (*Matthew* 10: 33; cp. *Mark* 8: 38; *Luke* 9: 26). But it must always be remembered that the New Testament tells of the terrible denial of Peter and of his gracious restoration. As so often happens, Jesus was gentler and more sympathetic and understanding than his Church was.

(*c*) It could be argued from this very letter of John that the most deadly of all sins was to deny that Jesus really came in the flesh, for that sin was nothing less than the mark of Antichrist (1 *John* 4: 3). If the mortal sin is to be identified with any one sin that surely must be it. But we think that there is something more to it even than that.

THE ESSENCE OF SIN

1 *John* 5: 16, 17 (*continued*)

FIRST of all, let us try to fix more closely the meaning of the *mortal sin*. In the Greek it is the sin *pros thanaton*. That means *the sin which is going towards death*, the sin whose end is death, the sin which, if continued in, must finish in death. The terrible thing about it is not so much what it is in itself, as where it will end, if a man persists in it.

It is a fact of experience that there are two kinds of sinners. On the one hand, there is the man who may be said to sin against his will; he sins because he is swept away by passion or desire, which at the moment is too strong for him; his sin is not so much a matter of choice as of a compulsion which he is not able to resist. On the other hand, there is the man who sins deliberately, of set purpose taking his own way, although well aware that it is wrong.

Now these two men began by being the same man. It is the experience of every man that the first time that he does a wrong thing, he does it with shrinking and with fear; and, after he has done it, he feels grief and remorse and regret. But, if he allows himself again and again to flirt with temptation and to fall, on each occasion the sin becomes easier; and, if he thinks he escapes the consequences, on each occasion the self-disgust and the remorse and the regret become less and less; and in the end he reaches a state when he can sin without a tremor. It is precisely that which is the sin which is leading to death. So long as a man in his heart of hearts hates sin and hates himself for sinning, so long as he *knows* that he is sinning, he is never beyond repentance and, therefore, never beyond forgiveness; but once he begins to revel in sin and to make it the deliberate policy of his life, he is on the way to death, for he is on the way to a state where the idea of repentance will not, and cannot, enter his head.

The mortal sin is the state of the man who has listened to sin and refused to listen to God so often, that he loves his sin and regards it as the most profitable thing in the world.

THE THREEFOLD CERTAINTY

1 *John* 5: 18-20

> We know that he who has received his birth from God does not sin, but he whose birth was from God keeps him, and the Evil One does not touch him.
>
> We know that it is from God that we draw our being, and the whole world lies in the power of the Evil One.
>
> We know that the Son of God has come, and that he has given us discernment to come to know the Real One; and we are in the Real One, even through his Son Jesus Christ. This is the real God and this is eternal life.

JOHN draws to the end of his letter with a statement of the threefold Christian certainty.

(i) The Christian is emancipated from the power of sin. We must be careful to see what this means. It does not mean that the Christian never sins; but it does mean that he is not the helpless slave of sin. As Plummer put it: "A child of God may sin, but his normal condition is resistance to evil." The difference lies in this. The pagan world was conscious of nothing so much as moral defeat. It knew its own evil and felt there was no possible escape. Seneca spoke of "our weakness in necessary things." He said that men "hate their sins but cannot leave them." Persius, the Roman satirist, in a famous picture spoke of "filthy Natta, a man deadened by vice . . . who has no sense of sin, no knowledge of what he is losing, and is sunk so deep that he sends up no bubble to the surface." The pagan world was utterly defeated by sin.

But the Christian is the man who never can lose the battle. Because he is a man, he will sin; but he never can experience the utter moral defeatedness of the pagan. F. W. H. Myers makes Paul speak of the battle with the flesh:

> "Well, let me sin, but not with my consenting,
> Well, let me die, but willing to be whole:
> Never, O Christ—so stay me from relenting—
> Shall there be truce betwixt my flesh and soul."

The reason for the Christian's ultimate undefeatedness is that *he who has his birth from God* keeps him. That is to say, Jesus keeps him. As Wescott has it: "The Christian has an active enemy, but he has also a watchful guardian." The heathen is the man who has been defeated by sin and has accepted defeat. The Christian is the man who may sin but never accepts the fact of defeat. "A saint," as someone has said, "is not a man who never falls; he is a man who gets up and goes on every time he falls."

(ii) The Christian is on the side of God against the world. The source of our being is God, but the world lies in the power of the Evil One. In the early days the cleavage between the Church and the world was much clearer than it is now. At least in the Western world, we live in a civilization permeated by Christian principles. Even if men do not practise them, they still, on the whole, accept the ideals of chastity, mercy, service, love. But the ancient world knew nothing of chastity, and little of mercy, and of service, and of love. John says that the Christian knows that he is with God, while the world is in the grip of the Evil One. No matter how the situation may have changed, the choice still confronts men whether they will align themselves with God or with the forces which are against God. As Myers makes Paul say:

> "Whoso hath felt the Spirit of the Highest,
> Cannot confound nor doubt him nor deny:
> Yea with one voice, O World, tho' thou deniest,
> Stand thou on that side, for on this am I."

(iii) The Christian is conscious that he has entered into that reality which is God. Life is full of illusions and impermanencies; by himself man can but guess and grope; but in Christ he enters into the knowledge of reality. Xenophon tells of a discussion between Socrates and a young man. "How do you know that?" says Socrates. "Do you know it, or are you guessing?" "I am guessing," is the answer. "Very well," says Socrates, "when we are done with guessing and when we know, shall we talk about it then?" Who am I? What is life? What is God? Whence did I come? Whither do I go? What is truth and where is duty? These are the questions to which men can reply only in guesses apart from Jesus Christ. But in Christ we reach the reality, which is God. The time of guessing is gone and the time of knowing has come.

THE CONSTANT PERIL

1 *John* 5:21

> My dear children, guard yourselves from idols.

With this sudden, sharp injunction John brings his letter to an end. Short as it is, there is a world of meaning in this phrase.

(i) In Greek the word *idol* has in it the sense of unreality. Plato used it for the illusions of this world as opposed to the unchangeable realities of eternity. When the prophets spoke of the idols of the heathen, they meant that they were counterfeit gods, as opposed to the one true God. This may well mean, as Westcott has it, "Keep yourselves from all objects of false devotion."

(ii) An idol is anything in this life which men worship instead of God and allow to take the place of God. A man may make an idol of his money, of his career, of his safety, of his pleasure. Again to quote Westcott: "An idol is anything which occupies the place due to God."

(iii) It is likely that John means something more definite than either of these two things. It was in Ephesus that he was writing, and it was of conditions in Ephesus that he was thinking. It is likely that he means simply and directly, "Keep yourselves from the pollutions of heathen worship."

No town in the world had so many connections with the stories of the ancient gods; and no town was more proud of them. Tacitus writes of Ephesus: "The Ephesians claimed that Diana and Apollo were not born at Delos, as was commonly supposed; they possessed the Cenchrean stream and the Ortygian grove where Latona, in travail, had reposed against an olive tree, which is still in existence, and had given birth to these deities. . . . It was there that Apollo himself, after slaying the Cyclops, had escaped the wrath of Jupiter: and again that father Bacchus in his victory had spared the suppliant Amazons who had occupied his shrine."

Further, in Ephesus there stood the great Temple of Diana, one of the wonders of the ancient world. There were at least three things about that Temple which would justify John's stern injunction to have nothing to do with heathen worship.

(a) The Temple was the centre of immoral rites. The priests were called the *Megabyzi*. They were eunuchs. It was said by some that the goddess was so fastidious that she could not bear a real male near her; it was said by others that the goddess was so lascivious that it was unsafe for any real male to approach her. Heraclitus, the great philosopher, was a native of Ephesus. He was called the weeping philosopher, for he had never been known to smile. He said that the darkness to the approach of the altar of the Temple was the darkness of vileness; that the morals of the Temple were worse than the morals of beasts; that the inhabitants of Ephesus were fit only to be drowned, and that the reason that he could never smile was that he lived in the midst of such terrible uncleanness. For a Christian to have any contact with that was to touch infection.

(b) The Temple had the right of asylum. Any criminal, if he could reach the Temple of Diana, was safe. The result was that the Temple was the haunt of criminals. Tacitus accused Ephesus of protecting the crimes of men and calling it the worship of the gods. To have anything to do with the Temple of Diana was to be associated with the very dregs of society.

(c) The Temple of Diana was the centre of the sale of Ephesian letters. These were charms, worn as amulets, which were supposed to be effective in bringing about the wishes of those who wore them. Ephesus was "pre-eminently the city of astrology, sorcery, incantations, amulets, exorcisms, and every form of magical imposture." To have anything to do with the Temple at Ephesus was to be brought into contact with commercialized superstition and the black arts.

It is hard for us to imagine how much Ephesus was dominated by the Temple of Diana. It would not be easy for a Christian to keep himself from idols in a city like that. But John demands that it must be done. The Christian must never be lost in the illusions of pagan religion; he must never erect in his heart an idol which will take the place of God; he must keep himself from the infections of all false faiths; and he can do so only when he walks with Christ.

INTRODUCTION TO THE
SECOND AND THIRD LETTERS OF JOHN

THE very shortness of these two letters is the best guarantee of their genuineness. They are so brief and so comparatively unimportant that no one would have gone to the trouble of inventing them and of attaching them to the name of John. A standard papyrus sheet measured ten by eight inches and the length of these letters is to be explained by the fact that they would each take up almost exactly one sheet.

THE ELDER

Each of them is said to come from "The elder." *Second John* begins: "The elder to the elect lady and her children." *Third John* begins: "The elder to the beloved Gaius." It is in the last degree unlikely that *The elder* is an official or ecclesiastical title. Elders were officials attached to one congregation whose jurisdiction did not extend outside that congregation, whereas the writer of these letters certainly assumes that he has the right to speak and that his word will carry weight in congregations where he is not actually present. He speaks as one whose authority goes out to the Church at large. The word is *presbuteros*, which originally meant *an elder*, not in the official but in the natural sense of the term. We would be better to translate it *The ancient*, or *The aged*, for it is not from an ecclesiastical position but from his age and personal qualities that the writer of these letters draws his authority.

In fact we know that in Ephesus there was an aged John who held a very special position. In the days of the early church there was a churchman called Papias who lived from A.D. 70 to 146. He had a passion for collecting all the information he could lay hands on about the early days of the church. He was not a great scholar, Eusebius dismisses him as "a man of very limited intelligence"; but he does transmit to us some most interesting information. He became Bishop of Hierapolis but he had a close connection with

Ephesus, and he tells us of his own methods of acquiring information. He frequently uses *elder* in the sense of *one of the fathers of the Church*, and he mentions a particularly distinguished *elder* whose name was John. "I shall not hesitate," he writes, "to put down for you, along with my own interpretations, whatsoever things I have at any time learned carefully from the *elders*, and carefully remembered, guaranteeing their truth. For I did not, like the multitude, take pleasure in those that speak much, but in those that teach the truth; not in those who relate strange commandments, but in those who deliver the commandments given by the Lord to faith, and springing from the truth itself. If, then, anyone came who had been a follower of the *elders*, I questioned him in regard to the words of the *elders*—what Andrew, or what Peter, had said, or what was said by Philip, or by Thomas, or by James, or by John, or by Matthew, or by any other of the disciples of the Lord; and what things Aristion, or the *Elder John* say. For I did not think that what was to be gotten from books would profit me as much as what came from the living and abiding voice." Clearly the *Elder John*, John the aged, was a notable figure in Ephesus, although he is clearly distinguished from John the apostle.

It must be this John who wrote these two little letters. By this time he was an old man, one of the last surviving links with Jesus and his disciples. He was a man who had the authority of a bishop in Ephesus and in the places around it; and when he saw that a church was threatened with trouble and heresy, he wrote with gracious and loving correction to his people. Here are the letters of an aged saint, one of the last of the first generation of Christians, a man whom all loved and respected.

COMMON AUTHORSHIP

That the two·letters are from the one hand there is no doubt. Short as they are, they have much in common. *Second John* begins: "The elder to the elect lady and her children, whom I love in the truth." *Third John* begins: "The elder to the beloved Gaius, whom I love in the truth." *Second John* goes on: "I rejoiced greatly to find some of your children following the truth" (verse 4); and *Third John* goes on: "No greater joy can I have than this, to hear that my children follow the truth." *Second John* comes to an end: "Though I have much to write to you, I would rather not use paper and ink, but I hope to come to see you and talk with you face to face, so that our joy may be complete" (verse 12). *Third John* comes to an end: "I had much to write to you, but I would rather not write with pen and ink; I hope to see you soon, and we will talk together face to face" (verses 13, 14). There is the closest possible similarity between the two letters.

There is further the closest possible connection between the situation of these letters and that in *First John*. In 1 *John* 4: 3 we read: "Every spirit which does not confess Jesus is not of God. This is the spirit of Antichrist, of which you heard that it was coming, and now it is in the world already." In 2 *John* 7 we read: "Many deceivers have gone out into the world, men who will not acknowledge the coming of Jesus Christ in the flesh; such a one is a deceiver and the Antichrist."

It is clear that *Second* and *Third John* are closely connected with each other; and that both are closely connected with *First John*. They are dealing with the same situation, the same dangers and the same people.

THE PROBLEM OF THE SECOND LETTER

These two little letters confront us with few serious problems. The only real one is to decide whether the Second Letter was sent to an individual or to a church. It begins: "The elder to the elect lady and her children." The problem centres on this phrase *the elect lady*. The Greek is *eklektē kuria* and there are three possible ways of taking it.

(i) It is just barely possible, though not really likely, that *Eklektē* is a proper name and that *kuria* is a quite usual affectionate address. *Kurios* (the masculine form) has many meanings. It very commonly means *sir*; it means *master* of slaves and *owner* of possessions; on a much higher level it means *lord* and is the word so often used as a title for Jesus. In letters *kurios* has a special use. It is practically the equivalent of the English phrase *My Dear*. So a soldier writes home saying, *Kurie mou patēr*, My Dear Father. In letters *kurios* is an address combining affection and respect. So it is just possible that this letter is addressed to *My Dear Eklektē*. Rendel Harris, indeed, went the length of saying that *Second John* is nothing other than a Christian love letter. This is unlikely, as we shall see, for more than one reason. But one thing is decisive against it. *Second John* ends: "The children of your elect sister greet you." The Greek is again *eklektē*; and, if it is a proper name at the beginning of the letter, it must also be a proper name at the end. This would mean that there were two sisters both called by the very unusual name of *Eklektē*—which is simply unbelievable.

(ii) It is possible to take *Kuria* as a proper name, for there are examples of this usage. We would then take *eklektē* in its normal New Testament sense; and the letter would be written to the *elect Kuria*. The objections are threefold. (*a*) It seems unlikely that any single individual could be spoken of as loved by all those who have known the truth (verse 1). (*b*) Verse 4 says that John rejoiced when he found some of her children walking in the truth; the implication is that others did not so walk. This would seem to imply a number greater than one woman's family could contain. (*c*) The decisive objection is that throughout the letter the *eklektē kuria* is addressed sometimes in the singular and sometimes in the plural. The singular occurs in verses 4, 5 and 13; and the plural occurs in verses 6, 8, 10, 12. It would be almost impossible that an individual would be so addressed.

(iii) So, then, we must come to the conclusion that *the elect lady* means *a church*. There is, in fact, good evidence that the expression was so used. *First Peter*, in the Authorized Version, ends with greetings from "the church that is at

Babylon elected together with you" (1 *Peter* 5: 13). In the Authorized Version the words *church that is* are in italics; that, of course, means that they are not in the Greek and have been supplied in translation to fill out the sense. The Greek literally reads: "The Elect One at Babylon" and *The Elect One* is feminine. Few have ever doubted that the phrase means *The church which is at Babylon*, and that is how we must take it in John's letter also. No doubt The Elect Lady goes back to the idea of the church as the Bride of Christ. We can be certain that *Second John* is written, not to an individual but to a church.

THE PROBLEM IN THE EARLY CHURCH

Second and *Third John* throw vivid light on a problem which sooner or later had to arise within the organization of the early church. Let us see if we can reconstruct the situation which lies behind them. It is clear that John the aged regards himself as having a right to act as guide and counsellor and to administer warning and rebuke in the churches whose members are his children. In *Second John* he writes of those who are doing well (verse 4), and by implication infers that there are others who are not so satisfactory. He further makes it clear that there are itinerant teachers in the district, some of whom are preaching false and dangerous doctrine, and he gives orders that such teachers are not to be accepted and not to be given hospitality (verses 7–11). Here, then, John is exercising what is to him an unquestioned right to issue orders to his churches and is seeking to guard against a situation in which itinerant teachers of falsehood may arrive at any moment.

The situation behind *Third John* is somewhat more complicated. The letter is written to one called Gaius, whose character and actions John most thoroughly approves (verses 3–5). Wandering missionaries have come to the church, men who are fellow-helpers of the truth, and Gaius has given them true Christian hospitality (verses 6–8). In the same church is another man called Diotrephes, who loves to have the preeminence (verse 9). Diotrephes is depicted as a dictatorial character who will brook no rival to his authority. Diotrephes has refused to receive the wandering teachers of the truth and has actually tried to drive out of the church those who did receive them. He will have nothing to do with wandering teachers even when they are true preachers of the word (verse 10). Then into the picture comes a man called Demetrius, to whom John gives a personal testimonial as a good man and one to be hospitably welcomed (verse 12). The simplest explanation of Demetrius is that he must be the leader of a wandering band of teachers who are on their way to the church to which John is writing. Diotrephes will certainly refuse to have anything to do with them and will try to eject those who do receive them; and John is writing to urge Gaius to receive the wandering teachers and not to be intimidated by the domineering Diotrephes, whom he (John) will deal with when he visits the church in question (verse 10). The whole situation turns on the reception of the wandering teachers. Gaius has received such teachers before, and John urges him to receive them and their leader Demetrius again. Diotrephes has shut the door on them and defied the authority of John the aged.

THE THREEFOLD MINISTRY

All this looks like a very unhappy situation, and indeed it was. None the less, it was one which was bound to arise. In the nature of things a problem of ministry was bound to emerge within the church. In its earliest days the church had three different kinds of ministries.

(i) Unique, and above all others, stood the *apostles*, those who had companied with Jesus and been witnesses of the resurrection. They were the undisputed leaders of the church. Their writ ran throughout the whole church; in any country and in any congregation their ministry was supreme.

(ii) There were the *prophets*. They were not attached to any one congregation. They were wandering preachers, going where the Spirit moved them and giving to men the message which the Spirit of God gave to them. They had given up home and occupation and the comfort and security of settled life to be the wandering messengers of God. They, too, had a very special place in the church. *The Didachē*, or, to give it its English name, *The Teaching of the Twelve Apostles*, is the earliest book of church order. In it the unique position of the prophets is made clear. The order of service for the Eucharist is laid down and the prayers are given; the service ends with the prayer of thanksgiving which is given in full; and then comes the sentence: "But suffer the prophets to give thanks as much as they will" (*Didachē* 10: 7). The prophets were not to be brought under the rules and regulations which governed ordinary people. So, then, the church had two sets of people whose authority was not confined to any one congregation and who had right of entry to every congregation.

(iii) There were the *elders*. During their first missionary journey part of the work of Paul and Barnabas was to ordain elders in all the local churches which they founded (*Acts* 14: 23). The elders were the officials of the settled community; their work was within their congregation and they did not move outside it. It is clear that they were the backbone of the organization of the early church; on them the routine work and the solidity of the individual congregations depended.

THE PROBLEM OF THE WANDERING PREACHERS

The position of the apostles presented no real problem; they were unique and their position could never really be disputed. But the wandering prophets did present a problem. Their position was one which was singularly liable to abuse. They had an enormous prestige; and it was possible for the most undesirable characters to enter into a way of life in which they moved from place to place, living in very considerable comfort at the expense of the local congregations. A clever rogue could make a very comfortable living as an itinerant prophet. Even the pagan satirists saw this. Lucian, the Greek writer, in his work called the *Peregrinus*, draws the picture

of a man who had found the easiest possible way of making
a living without working. He was an itinerant charlatan who
lived on the fat of the land by travelling round the various
communities of the Christians, settling down wherever he liked
and living luxuriously at their expense. *The Didachē* clearly
saw this danger and laid down definite regulations to meet
it. The regulations are long but so vivid a light do they
throw on the life of the early church that they are worth
quoting in full (*Didachē* 11 and 12).

Whosoever, therefore, shall come and teach you all these things
aforesaid, receive him. But if the teacher himself turn and teach
another doctrine to pervert, hear him not. But unto the increase
of righteousness and knowledge of the Lord, receive him as the
Lord. And as touching the apostles and prophets, according to the
decree of the gospel, so do ye. But let every apostle that cometh
unto you be received as the Lord. And he shall stay one day, and,
if need be, the next also, but, if he stay three, he is a false
prophet. And, when the apostle goeth forth, let him take nothing
save bread, till he reach his lodging, but, if he ask money, he is a
false prophet. And every prophet that speaketh in the Spirit ye
shall not try nor judge: for every sin shall be forgiven, but this
sin shall not be forgiven. But not everyone that speaketh in the
Spirit is a prophet, but if he has the manners of the Lord. By their
manners, therefore, shall the prophet and the false prophet be
known. And no prophet who ordereth a table in the Spirit shall eat
of it, else he is a false prophet. And every prophet that teacheth
the truth, if he doeth not what he teacheth, is a false prophet. . . .
Whosoever shall say in the Spirit: Give me money, or any other
thing, ye shall not hearken to him: but, if he bid you give for
others who are in need, let no man judge him.

Let everyone that cometh in the name of the Lord be received,
and then, when ye have proved him, ye shall know, for ye shall
have understanding to distinguish between the right hand and the
left. If he that cometh is a passer-by, succour him as far as ye can;
but he shall not stay with you longer than two or three days, unless
there be necessity. But, if he be minded to settle among you, and
be a craftsman, let him work and eat. But, if he hath no trade,
according to your understanding, provide that he shall not live idle
among you, being a Christian. But, if he will not do this, he is a
Christmonger: of such men beware.

The Didachē even invents the word *Christmonger, trafficker in Christ, Christemporos,* to describe this kind of person.

John was entirely justified in warning his people that the wrong kind of wandering prophets might come claiming hospitality and in saying that they must on no account be received. There is no doubt that in the early church these wandering prophets became a problem. Some of them were heretical teachers, even if they were sincerely convinced of their own teaching. Some were nothing better than plausible rogues who had found an easy way to make a comfortable living. That is the picture which lies behind *Second John.*

THE CLASH OF MINISTRIES

But the situation behind *Third John* is in some ways even more serious. The problem figure is Diotrephes. He is the man who will have nothing to do with wandering teachers and who seeks to eject anyone who dares to give them a welcome. He is the man who will not accept the authority of John and whom John brands as a domineering character. There is much more behind this than meets the eye. This was no storm in a tea-cup; it was a fundamental cleavage between the local and the itinerant ministry.

Obviously the whole structure of the church depended on a strong settled ministry. That is to say, its very existence depended on a strong and authoritative eldership. As time went on the settled ministry was bound to chafe under the remote control of even one so famous as John the aged; and to resent the possibly upsetting invasions of wandering prophets and evangelists. It was by no means impossible that, however well-intentioned they were, these itinerants could do far more harm than good.

Here is the situation behind *Third John.* John represents the old apostolic remote control; Demetrius and his band of missionaries represent the wandering prophets and preachers; Diotrephes represents the settled ministry of the local elders, who wish to run their own congregation and regard the wandering preachers as dangerous intruders; Gaius represents the good, well-meaning man who is torn in two and cannot make up his mind.

What happened in this case, we do not know. But the end of the matter in the church was that the wandering preachers faded from the scene and the apostles in the nature of things passed from this earth, and the settled ministry became the ministry of the church. In a sense even in the modern church the problem of the itinerant evangelist and the settled ministry is not fully solved; but these two little letters are of the most fascinating interest because they show the organization of the church in a transition stage, when the clash between the itinerant and the settled ministry was beginning to emerge and—who knows?—Diotrephes may not have been as bad as he is painted nor altogether wrong.

2 JOHN

THE ELECT LADY

2 *John* 1–3

> The Elder to the Elect Lady and to her children, whom I love
> in truth (it is not only I who love you and them, but so do all
> who love the truth) because of the truth which abides in us and
> which will be with us for ever. Grace, mercy and peace will be
> with you from God the Father and from Jesus Christ the Son
> of the Father, in truth and love.

THE writer designates himself simply by the title of The Elder
Elder can have three different meanings.

(i) It can mean simply *an older man*, one who by reason
of his years and experience is deserving of affection and of
respect. There will be something of that meaning here. The
letter is from an aged servant of Christ and the church.

(ii) In the New Testament the elders are the *officials of the
local churches*. They were the first of all the church officials,
and Paul ordained elders in his churches on his missionary
journeys, as soon as it was possible to do so (*Acts* 14: 21–23).
The word cannot be used in that sense here, because these
elders were local officials, whose authority and duties were
confined to their own congregation, whereas The Elder of this
letter clearly has an authority which extends over a much
wider area. He claims the right to advise congregations in
places where he himself is not a resident.

(iii) Almost certainly this letter was written in Ephesus in
the province of Asia. In the church there *Elder* was used
in a special sense. The elders were men who had been direct
disciples of the apostles; it is from these men that both Papias
and Irenaeus, who lived and worked and wrote in Asia, tell
us that they got their information. The elders were the direct
links between the second generation of Christians and the
followers of Christ in the flesh. It is undoubtedly in that sense
that the word is used here. The writer of the letter is one of

the last direct links with Jesus Christ; and therein lies his right to speak.

As we have already said in the introduction, *The Elect Lady* is something of a problem. There are two suggestions.

(i) There are those who hold that the letter is written to *an individual person*. In Greek the phrase is *Eklektē Kuria*. *Kurios* (the masculine form of the adjective) is a common form of respectful address and *Eklektē* could just possibly—though not probably—be a proper name, in which case the letter would be written to *My Dear Eklektē*. *Kuria*, besides being a title of respectful address, can be a proper name, in which case *eklektē* would be an adjective and the letter would be to *The Elect Kuria*. Just possibly *both* words are proper names, in which case the letter would be to a lady called *Eklektē Kuria*.

But, if this letter is written to an individual, it is much more likely that *neither* word is a proper name and that the Revised Standard Version is correct in translating the phrase *The elect lady*. There has been much speculation as to who The Elect Lady might be. We mention only two of the suggestions. (*a*) It has been suggested that *The Elect Lady* is Mary, the mother of our Lord. She was to be a mother to John and he was to be a son to her (*John* 19: 26, 27), and a personal letter from John might well be a letter to her. (*b*) *Kurios* means *Master*; and *Kuria* as a proper name would mean *Mistress*. In Latin, *Domina* is the same name and in Aramaic, *Martha*; both meaning *Mistress* or *Lady*. It has, therefore, been suggested that the letter was written to Martha of Bethany.

(ii) It is much more likely that the letter is written to a *church*. It is far more likely that it is a church which all men love who know the truth (verse 1). Verse 4 says that some of the children are walking in the truth. In verses 4, 8, 10, 12 the word *you* is in the plural, which suggests a church. Peter uses almost exactly the same phrase when he sends greetings from The Elect One (the form is feminine) which is at Babylon (1 *Peter* 5: 13).

It may well be that the address is deliberately un-identifiable. The letter was written at a time when persecution was a real possibility. If it were to fall into the wrong hands, there might well be trouble. And it may be that the letter is addressed in such a way that to the insider its destination is quite clear, while to the outsider it would look like a personal letter from one friend to another.

LOVE AND TRUTH

2 John 1–3 (*continued*)

IT is of great interest to note how in this passage *love* and *truth* are inseparably connected. It is *in the truth* that the elder loves the elect lady. It is *because of the truth* that he loves and writes to the church. In Christianity we learn two things about love.

(i) Christian truth tells us the way in which we ought to love. *Agapē* is the word for Christian love. *Agapē* is not passion with its ebb and flow, its flicker and its flame; nor is it an easy-going and indulgent sentimentalism. And it is not an easy thing to acquire or a light thing to exercise. *Agapē* is undefeatable goodwill; it is the attitude towards others which, no matter what they do, will never feel bitterness and will always seek their highest good. There is a love which seeks to possess; there is a love which softens and enervates; there is a love which withdraws a man from the battle; there is a love which shuts its eyes to faults and to ways which end in ruin. But Christian love will always seek the highest good of others and will accept all the difficulties, all the problems and all the toil which that search involves. It is of significance that John writes in love to warn.

(ii) Christian truth tells us the reason for the obligation of love. In his first letter, John clearly lays it down. He has talked of the suffering, sacrificing, incredibly generous love of God; and then he says, "Beloved, if God so loved us, we ought also to love one another" (1 *John* 4: 11). *The*

Christian must love because he is loved. He cannot accept the love of God without showing love to the men God loves. Because God loves us, we must love others with the same generous and sacrificial love.

Before we leave this passage we must note one other thing. John begins this letter with a greeting, but it is a very unusual greeting. He says, "Grace, mercy and peace will be with us." In every other New Testament letter the greeting is in the form of a wish or a prayer. Paul usually says, "Grace be to you and peace." Peter says, "May grace and peace be multiplied to you" (1 *Peter* 1:2). Jude says, "May mercy, peace and love, be multiplied to you" (*Jude* 2). But here the greeting is a *statement*: "Grace, mercy and peace *will be* with us." John is so sure of the gifts of the grace of God in Jesus Christ that he does not pray that his friends should receive them; he assures them that they will receive them. Here is the faith which never doubts the promises of God in Jesus Christ.

TROUBLE AND CURE

2 John 4-6

It gave me great joy to find some of your children walking in the truth, as we have received commandment from the Father. And now, Lady, not as if I were writing a new commandment to you, but a commandment which we have had from the beginning, I beg you that we should love one another. And this is love, that we should walk according to his commandments; and this is the commandment, as you have heard from the beginning, that we should walk in it.

In the church to which he is writing there are things to make John's heart glad and things to make it sad. It brings him joy to know that some of its members are walking in the truth; but that very statement implies that some are not. That is to say, within the church there is division, for there are those who have chosen to walk different roads. For all things John has one remedy and that is love. It is no new remedy and no new commandment; it is the word of Jesus himself: "A new commandment I give to you, that you love one another; even as I have loved you, that you also love one another. By this all men will know that you are my disciples, if you have love for one another" (*John* 13: 34, 35). Only love can mend a situation in which personal relationships are broken. Rebuke and criticism are liable to awaken only resentment and hostility; argument and controversy are liable only to widen the breach; love is the one thing to heal the breach and restore the lost relationship.

But it is possible that those who, as John sees it, have gone the wrong way might say, "We do indeed love God." Immediately John's thoughts go to another saying of Jesus: "If you love me, you will keep my commandments" (*John* 14: 15). Jesus's actual commandment was to love one another and, therefore, anyone who does not keep this commandment does not really love God, however much he may claim to do so. The only proof of our love for God is our love for the brethren. This is the commandment, says John, which we have heard from the beginning and in which we must walk.

As we go on we shall see that there is another side to this and that there is no soft sentimentality in John's attitude towards those who were seducing men from the truth; but it is significant that his first cure for all the troubles of the church is love.

THE THREATENING PERIL

2 John 7–9

> There is all the more reason to speak like this because there have gone out into the world many deceivers, men who do not confess that Jesus is Christ, and his coming in the flesh. Such a man is the deceiver and the Antichrist. Look to yourselves that you do not ruin that which we have wrought, but see to it that you

receive a full reward. Everyone who advances too far and who
does not abide in the teaching of Christ, does not possess God;
it is he who abides in that teaching who has both the Father and
the Son.

ALREADY, in *John* 4: 2, John has dealt with the heretics who
deny the reality of the incarnation. There is one difficulty.
In 1 *John* 4: 2 the Greek is that Jesus *has* come in the flesh.
The idea is expressed in a participle and the participle is in
the past tense. It is the fact that the incarnation has happened
which is stressed. Here there is a change and the participle
is in the present tense: the literal translation would be that
Jesus *comes* or *is coming* in the flesh. As far as the language
goes this could mean either of two things.

(i) It could mean that Jesus is always coming in the flesh,
that there is a kind of permanence about the incarnation,
that it was not one act which finished in the thirty years
during which Jesus was in Palestine but is timeless. That would
be a great thought and would mean that now and always
Jesus Christ, and God through him, is entering into the human
situation and into human life.

(ii) It could be a reference to the *Second Coming*; and it
could mean that Jesus is *coming again* in the flesh. It may
well be that there was a belief in the early church that there
was to be a second coming of Jesus in the flesh, a kind of
incarnation in glory to follow the incarnation of humiliation.
That, too, would be a great thought.

But it may well be that C. H. Dodd is right when he says
that in a late Greek writer like John, who did not know
Greek as the great classical writers knew it, we cannot lay all
this stress on tenses; and that we are better to take it that
he means the same as he meant in 1 *John* 4: 2. That is, these
deceivers are denying the reality of the incarnation and therefore denying that God can fully enter into the life of man.

It is intensely significant to note how the great thinkers
held on with both hands to the reality of the incarnation.
In the second century, again and again Ignatius insists that

Jesus was *truly* born, that he *truly* became man, that he *truly* suffered and that he *truly* died. Vincent Taylor, in his book on *The Person of Christ*, reminds us of two great statements of the incarnation. Martin Luther said of Jesus: "He ate, drank, slept, waked; was weary, sorrowful, rejoicing; he wept and he laughed; he knew hunger and thirst and sweat; he talked, he toiled, he prayed . . . so that there was no difference between *him* and other men, save only this, that he was *God*, and had no sin." Emil Brunner cites that passage, and then goes on to say, "The Son of God in whom we are able to believe must be such a One that it is possible to mistake him for an ordinary man."

If God could enter into life only as a disembodied phantom, the body stands for ever despised; then there can be no real communion between the divine and the human; then there can be no real salvation. He had to become what we are to make us what he is.

In verses 8 and 9 we hear beneath the words of John the claims of the false teachers.

It is their claim that they are *developing* Christianity discovering more truly what it means. John insists that they are destroying Christianity and wrecking the foundation which has been laid and on which everything must be built.

Verse 9 is interesting and significant. We have translated the first phrase *everyone who goes too far*. The Greek is *proagōn*. The verb means *to go on ahead*. The false teachers claimed that they were the progressives, the advanced thinkers, the men of the open and adventurous mind. John himself was one of the most adventurous thinkers of the New Testament. But he insists that, however far a man may advance, he must abide in the teaching of Jesus Christ or he loses touch with God. Here, then, is the great truth. John is not condemning advanced thinking; but he is saying that Jesus Christ must be the touchstone of all thinking and that whatever is out of touch with him can never be right. John would say, "Think—but take your thinking to the touchstone of Jesus Christ and the New Testament picture of him."

Christianity is not a nebulous, uncontrolled theosophy; it is anchored to the historical figure of Jesus Christ.

NO COMPROMISE

2 *John* 10–13

> If anyone comes to you and does not bring this teaching, do not receive him into your house and do not greet him on the street; for he who greets him becomes a partner in his evil deeds.
>
> Although I have many things to write to you, I do not wish to do so with paper and ink, but I hope to come to see you and to speak to you face to face, that our joy may be completed.
>
> The children of your Elect Sister send their greetings to you.

HERE we see very clearly the danger which John saw in these false teachers. They are to be given no hospitality; and the refusal of hospitality would be the most effective way of stopping their work. John goes further; they are not even to be given a greeting on the street. This would be to indicate that to some extent you had sympathy with them. It must be made quite clear to the world that the church has no tolerance for those whose teaching destroys the faith. This passage may seem on the face of it to run counter to Christian love; but C. H. Dodd has certain very wise things to say about it.

It is by no means without parallel. When the saintly Polycarp met the heretic Marcion, Marcion said: "Do you recognize me?" "I recognize Satan's first-born," answered Polycarp. It was John himself who fled from the public baths when Cerinthus, the heretic, entered them. "Let us hurry away lest the building collapse on us," he said, "because Cerinthus, the enemy of truth, is here."

We have to remember the situation. There was a time when it was touch and go whether the Christian faith would be destroyed by the speculations of pseudo-philosophic heretics. Its very existence was in peril. The church dared not even seem to compromise with this destructive corrosion of the faith.

This, as C. H. Dodd points out, is an emergency regulation and "emergency regulations make bad law." We may recognize the necessity of this way of action in the situation in which John and his people found themselves, without in the least holding that we must treat mistaken thinkers in the same way. And yet, to return to C. H. Dodd, a good-humoured tolerance can never be enough. "The problem is to find a way of living with those whose convictions differ from our own upon the most fundamental matters, without either breaking charity or being disloyal to the truth." It is there that love must find a way. The best way to destroy our enemies, as Abraham Lincoln said, is to make them our friends. We can never compromise with mistaken teachers but we are never free from the obligation of seeking to lead them into the truth.

So John comes to an end. He will not write any more for he hopes to come to see his friends and to speak to them face to face. Both Greek and Hebrew say, not *face to face*, but *mouth to mouth*. In the Old Testament God says of Moses: "With him I speak mouth to mouth" (*Numbers* 12: 8). John was wise and he knew that letters can often only bedevil a situation and that five minutes heart to heart talk can do what a whole file of letters is powerless to achieve. In many a church and in many a personal relationship, letters have merely succeeded in exacerbating a situation; for the most carefully written letter can be misinterpreted, when a little speech together might have mended matters. Cromwell never understood John Fox, the Quaker, and much disliked him. Then he met him, and after he had spoken to him, he said, "If you and I had but an hour together, we would be better friends than we are." Church courts and Christian people would do well to make a resolution never to write when they could speak.

The letter closes with greetings from John's church to the friends to whom he writes, greetings, as it were, from one sister's children to another's, for all Christians are members of one family in the faith.

3 JOHN

THE TEACHER'S JOY

3 John 1–4

> The Elder to Gaius, the beloved, whom I love in truth.
>
> Beloved, I pray that everything is going well with you, and that you are in good health of body, as it goes well with your soul. It gave me great joy when certain brothers came and testified of the truth of your life, as indeed you do walk in the truth. No news brings me greater joy than to hear that my children are walking in the truth.

No New Testament letter better shows that the Christian letters were exactly on the model which all letter-writers used in the time of the early church. There is a papyrus letter from Irenaeus, a ship's captain, to his brother Apolinarius:

> Irenaeus to Apolinarius his brother, my greetings. Continually I pray that you may be in health, even as I myself am in health. I wish you to know that I arrived at land on the 6th of the month Epeiph, and I finished unloading my ship on the 18th of the same month, and went up to Rome on the 25th of the same month, and the place welcomed us, as God willed. Daily we are waiting for our discharge, so that up till today no one of us in the corn service has been allowed to go. I greet your wife much, and Serenus, and all who love you, by name. Good bye.

The form of Irenaeus's letter is exactly that of John's. There is first the greeting, next the prayer for good health, after that the main body of the letter with its news, and then the final greetings. The early Christian letters were not something remote and ecclesiastical; they were the kind of letters which people wrote to each other every day.

John writes to a friend called Gaius. In the world of the New Testament Gaius was the commonest of all names. In the New Testament there are three men with that name. There is Gaius, the Macedonian who, along with Aristarchus, was with Paul at the riot in Ephesus (*Acts* 19: 29). There is Gaius of Derbe, who was the delegate of his church to convey the

collection for the poor to Jerusalem (*Acts* 20: 4). There is
the Gaius of Corinth who had been Paul's host, and who was
such a hospitable soul that he could be called the host of the
whole church (*Romans* 16: 23), and who was one of the very
few people whom Paul had personally baptized (1 *Corinthians*
1: 14), and who, according to tradition, became the first Bishop
of Thessalonica. Gaius was the commonest of all names; and
there is no reason to identify our Gaius with any of these three.
According to tradition he was made the Bishop of Pergamum
by John himself. Here he stands before us as a man with an
open house and an open heart.

Twice in the first two verses of this little letter John uses the
word *beloved*. (The *well-beloved* and *beloved* of the Authorized
Version's first two verses translate the same Greek word,
agapētos.) In this group of letters John uses *agapētos* no fewer
than ten times. This is a very notable fact. These letters are
letters of warning and rebuke; and yet their accent is the accent
of love. It was the advice of a great scholar and preacher:
"Never scold your congregation." Even if he has to rebuke,
John never speaks with irritation. The whole atmosphere of
his writing is that of love.

Verse 2 shows us the comprehensive care of the good and
devoted pastor. John is interested both in the physical and the
spiritual health of Gaius. John was like Jesus; he never forgot
that men have bodies as well as souls and that they matter, too.

In verse 4 John tells us of the teacher's greatest joy. It is to
see his pupils walking in the truth. The truth is not simply
something to be intellectually assimilated; it is the knowledge
which fills a man's mind and the charity which clothes his life.
The truth is what makes a man think and act like God.

CHRISTIAN HOSPITALITY

3 *John* 5–8

Beloved, whatever service you render to the brothers, strangers as
they are, is an act of true faith and they testify to your love before
the church. It will be a further kindness, if you send them on their

way worthily of God. For they have gone out for the sake of the
Name and they take no assistance from pagans. It is a duty to
support such men, that we may show ourselves fellow-workers with
the truth.

HERE we come to John's main object in writing. A group of
travelling missionaries is on its way to the church of which
Gaius is a member, and John urges him to receive them, to
give them every support and to send them on their way in a
truly Christian manner.

In the ancient world hospitality was a sacred duty. Strangers
were under the protection of Zeus Xenios, Zeus the god of
strangers (*Xenos* is the Greek for a *stranger*). In the ancient
world inns were notoriously unsatisfactory. The Greek had an
instinctive dislike of taking money for the giving of hospitality;
and, therefore, the profession of innkeeper ranked very low.
Inns were notoriously dirty and flea-infested. Innkeepers were
notoriously rapacious so that Plato compared them to pirates
who hold their guests to ransom before they allow them to
escape. The ancient world had a system of *guest-friendships*
whereby families in different parts of the country undertook
to give each other's members hospitality when the occasion
arose. This connection between families lasted throughout the
generations and when it was claimed the claimant brought with
him a *sumbolon,* or *token,* which identified him to his hosts.
Some cities kept an official called the *Proxenos* in the larger
cities to whom their citizens, when travelling, might appeal for
shelter and for help.

If the heathen world accepted the obligation of hospitality,
it was only to be expected that the Christians would take it
even more seriously. It is Peter's injunction: "Practise hospitality ungrudgingly to one another" (1 *Peter* 4: 9). "Do not
neglect to show hospitality to strangers" says the writer to the
Hebrews, and adds: "for thereby some have entertained angels
unawares" (*Hebrews* 13: 2). In the Pastoral Epistles a widow
is to be honoured if she has "shown hospitality" (1 *Timothy*
5: 9). Paul bids the Romans to "practise hospitality"
(*Romans* 12: 13).

Hospitality was to be specially the characteristic of the leaders of the church. A bishop must be a man given to hospitality (1 *Timothy* 3: 2). Titus is told to be "hospitable" (*Titus* 1: 8). When we come down to the time of Justin Martyr (A.D. 170) we find that on the Lord's Day the well-to-do contributed as they would and it was the duty of the president of the congregation "to succour the orphans and the widows, and those who through sickness or any other cause are in want, and those who are in bonds, and the strangers sojourning amongst us" (Justin Martyr: *First Apology* 1: 67).

In the early church the Christian home was the place of the open door and the loving welcome. There can be few nobler works than to give a stranger the right of entry to a Christian home. The Christian family circle should always be wide enough to have a place for the stranger, no matter where he comes from or what his colour.

THE CHRISTIAN ADVENTURERS

3 John 5–8 (*continued*)

FURTHER, this passage tells us about the wandering missionaries who gave up home and comfort to carry afield the word of God. In verse 7 Paul says that they have gone forth for the sake of the Name and take no assistance from pagans. (It is just possible that verse 7 might refer to those who had come out from the Gentiles taking nothing with them, those who for the sake of Christianity had left their work and their home and their friends and had no means of support.) In the ancient world the "begging friar," with his wallet, was well known. There is, for instance, a record of a man calling himself "the slave of the Syrian goddess," who went out begging and claimed that he never came back with fewer than seventy bags of money for his goddess. But these Christian wandering preachers would take nothing from the Gentiles, even if they would have given it.

John commends these adventurers of the faith to the hospitality and the generosity of Gaius. He says that it is a duty to help them so that we may show ourselves fellow-workers in the truth (verse 8). Moffatt translates this very vividly: "We are bound to support such men to prove ourselves allies of the truth."

There is a great Christian thought here. A man's circumstances may be such that he cannot become a missionary or a preacher. Life may have put him in a position where he must get on with a secular job, staying in the one place and carrying out the routine duties of life and living. But where he cannot go, his money and his prayers and his practical support can go. Not everyone can be, so to speak, in the front line; but by supporting those who are there, he can make himself an ally of the truth. When we remember that, all giving to the wider work of Christ and his church must become not an obligation but a privilege, not a duty but a delight. The church needs those who will go out with the truth, but it also needs those who will be allies of the truth at home.

LOVE'S APPEAL

3 John 9–15

I have already written something to the church, but Diotrephes, who is ambitious for the leadership, does not accept our authority. So, then, when I come, I will bring up the matter of his actions, for he talks nonsensically about us with wicked words; he refuses to receive the brothers and attempts to stop those who wish to do so and tries to eject them from the church.

Beloved do not imitate the evil but the good. He who does good has the source of his life in God; he who does evil has not seen God.

Everybody testifies to the worth of Demetrius, and so does the truth itself; and so do we testify, and you know that our testimony is true.

I have many things to write to you; but I do not wish to write to you with ink and pen. I hope to see you soon, and we shall talk face to face.

Peace be to you. The friends send their greetings. Greet the friends by name.

HERE we come to the reason why this letter was written and

are introduced to two of the main characters in the story.

There is Diotrephes. In the introduction we have already seen the situation in which John and Diotrephes and Demetrius are all involved. In the early church there was a double ministry. There were the apostles and the prophets whose sphere was not confined to any one congregation and whose authority extended all over the church. There were also the elders; they were the permanent settled ministry of the local congregations and their very backbone.

In the early days this presented no problem, for the local congregations were still very much infants who had not yet learned to walk by themselves and to handle their own affairs. But as time went on there came a tension between the two kinds of ministry. As the local churches became stronger and more conscious of their identity, they inevitably became less and less willing to submit to remote control or to the invasion of itinerant strangers.

The problem is still to some extent with us. There is the itinerant evangelist who may well have a theology and work with methods and in an atmosphere very different from that of the settled local congregation. In the younger churches there is the question of how long the missionaries should remain in control and of when the time has come for them to withdraw and allow the indigenous churches to rule their own affairs.

In this letter Diotrephes is the representative of the local congregation. He will not accept the authority of John, the apostolic man and he will not receive the itinerant missionaries. He is so determined to see that the local congregation manages its own affairs that he will even eject those who are still prepared to accept the authority of John and to receive the wandering preachers. What exactly Diotrephes is we cannot tell. He certainly is not a bishop in anything like the modern sense of the word. He may be a very strong-minded elder. Or he may even be an aggressive member of the congregation who by the force of his personality is sweeping all before him. Certainly he emerges as a strong and dominant character.

Demetrius is most likely the leader of the wandering preachers and probably the actual bearer of this letter. John goes out of his way to give him a testimonial as to character and ability, and it may well be that there are certain circumstances attaching to him which give Diotrephes a handle for his opposition.

Demetrius is by no means an uncommon name. Attempts have been made to identify him with two New Testament characters. He has been identified with Demetrius, the silversmith of Ephesus and the leader of the opposition to Paul (*Acts* 19: 21ff.). It may be that he afterwards became a Christian and that his early opposition was still a black mark against him. He has been identified with Demas (a shortened form of *Demetrius*), who had once been one of Paul's fellow-labourers but who had forsaken him because he loved this present world (*Colossians* 4: 14; *Philemon* 24; 2 *Timothy* 4: 10). It may be that Demas came back to the faith and that his desertion of Paul was always held against him.

Into this situation comes John, whose authority is being flouted; and Gaius, a kindly soul but probably not so strong a character as the aggressive Diotrephes, whom John is seeking to align with himself, for Gaius, left on his own, might well succumb to Diotrephes.

There is our situation. We may have a good deal of sympathy with Diotrephes; we may well think that he was taking a stand which sooner or later had to be taken. But for all his strength of character he had one fault—he was lacking in charity. As C. H. Dodd has put it: "There is no real religious experience which does not express itself in charity." That is why, for all his powers of leadership and for all his dominance of character, Diotrephes was not a real Christian, as John saw it. The true Christian leader must always remember that strength and gentleness must go together and that leading and loving must go hand in hand. Diotrephes was like so many leaders in the church. He may well have been right, but he took the wrong way to achieve his end, for no amount of strength of mind can take the place of love of heart.

What the issue of all this was we do not know. But John comes to the end in love. Soon he will come and talk, when his presence will do what no letter can ever do; and for the present he sends his greetings and his blessing. And we may well believe that the "Peace be to you" of the aged Elder indeed brought calm to the troubled church to which he wrote.

THE LETTER OF JUDE

INTRODUCTION TO THE
LETTER OF JUDE

THE DIFFICULT AND NEGLECTED LETTER

IT may well be said that for the great majority of modern readers reading the little letter of Jude is a bewildering rather than a profitable undertaking. There are two verses which everyone knows—the resounding and magnificent doxology with which it ends:

> Now to him who is able to keep you from falling and to present you without blemish before the presence of his glory with rejoicing, to the only God our Saviour through Jesus Christ our Lord, be glory, majesty, dominion and authority, before all time and now and for ever. Amen.

But, apart from these two great verses, *Jude* is largely unknown and seldom read. The reason for its difficulty is that it is written out of a background of thought, against the challenge of a situation, in pictures and with quotations, which are all quite strange to us. Beyond a doubt it would hit those who read it for the first time like a hammer-blow. It would be like a trumpet call to defend the faith. Moffatt calls *Jude* "a fiery cross to rouse the churches." But, as J. B. Mayor, one of its greatest editors, has said: "To a modern reader it is curious rather than edifying with the exception of the beginning and the end."

This is one of the great reasons for addressing ourselves to the study of *Jude*; for, when we understand Jude's thought and disentangle the situation against which he was writing, his letter becomes of the greatest interest for the history of the earliest church and by no means without relevance for today. There have indeed been times in the history of the church, and especially in its revivals when *Jude* was not far from being the most relevant book in the New Testament. Let us begin by simply setting down the substance of the letter without waiting for the explanations which must follow later.

MEETING THE THREAT

It had been Jude's intention to write a treatise on the faith which all Christians share; but that task had to be laid aside in view of the rise of men whose conduct and thought were a threat to the Christian Church (verse 3). In view of this situation the need was not so much to expound the faith as to rally Christians in its defence. Certain men who had insinuated themselves into the church were busily engaged in turning the grace of God into an excuse for open immorality and were denying the only true God and Jesus Christ the Lord (verse 4). These men were immoral in life and heretical in belief.

THE WARNINGS

Against these men Jude marshals his warnings. Let them remember the fate of the Israelites. They had been brought in safety out of Egypt but they had never been permitted to enter the Promised Land because of their unbelief (verse 5). The reference is to *Numbers* 13: 26—14: 29. Although a man had received the grace of God, he might still lose his eternal salvation if he drifted into disobedience and unbelief. Some angels with the glory of heaven as their own had come to earth and corrupted mortal women with their lust (*Genesis* 6: 2); and now they were imprisoned in the abyss of darkness, awaiting judgment (verse 6). He who rebels against God must look for judgment. The cities of Sodom and Gomorrah had given themselves over to lust and to unnatural vice, and their destruction in flames is a dreadful warning to everyone who similarly goes astray (verse 7).

THE EVIL LIFE

These men are visionaries of evil dreams; they defile their flesh; and they speak evil of the angels (verse 8). Not even Michael the archangel, dare speak evil even of the evil angels. It had been given to Michael to bury the body of Moses. The devil had tried to stop him and claim the body for himself. Michael had spoken no evil against the devil, even in circumstances like that, but had simply said, "The Lord rebuke you!"

(verse 9). Angels must be respected, even when evil and hostile. These evil men condemn everything which they do not understand, and spiritual things are beyond their understanding. They do understand their fleshly instincts and allow themselves to be governed by them as the brute beasts do (verse 10).

They are like Cain, the cynical, selfish murderer; they are like Balaam, whose one desire was for gain and who led the people into sin; they are like Korah, who rebelled against the legitimate authority of Moses and was swallowed up by the earth for his arrogant disobedience (verse 11).

They are like the hidden rocks on which a ship may founder; they have their own clique in which they consort with people like themselves, and thus destroy Christian fellowship; they deceive others with their promises, like clouds which promise the longed-for rain and then pass over the sky; they are like fruitless and rootless trees, which have no harvest of good fruit; as the foaming spray of the waves casts the sea-weed and the wreckage on the beaches, they foam out shameless deeds; they are like disobedient stars who refuse to keep their appointed orbit and are doomed to the dark (verse 13). Long ago the prophet Enoch had described these men and had prophesied their divine destruction (verse 15). They murmur against all true authority and discipline as the children of Israel murmured against Moses in the desert; they are discontented with the lot which God has appointed to them; their lusts are their dictators; their speech is arrogant and proud; they are toadies of the great for sake of gain (verse 16).

VORDS TO THE FAITHFUL

Having castigated the evil men with this torrent of invective, Jude turns to the faithful. They could have expected all this to happen, for the apostles of Jesus Christ had foretold the rise of evil men (verses 18, 19). But the duty of the true Christian is to build his life on the foundation of the most holy faith; to learn to pray in the power of the Holy Spirit; to remember the conditions of the covenant into which the love of God has called him; to wait for the mercy of Jesus Christ (verses 20, 21).

As for the false thinkers and the loose livers—some of them may be saved with pity while they are still hesitating on the brink of their evil ways; others have to be snatched like brands from the burning; and, in all his rescue work, the Christian must have that godly fear which will love the sinner but hate the sin and must avoid the pollution of those he seeks to save (verses 22, 23).

And all the time there will be with him the power of that God who can keep him from falling and bring him pure and joyful into his presence (verses 24, 25).

THE HERETICS

Who were the heretics whom Jude blasts, and what were their beliefs and what their way of life? Jude never tells us. He was not a theologian but, as Moffatt says, "a plain, honest leader of the church." "He denounces rather than describes" the heresies he attacks. He does not seek to argue and to refute, for he writes as one "who knows when round indignation is more telling than argument." But from the letter itself we can deduce three things about these heretics.

(i) They were antinomians. Antinomians have existed in every age of the church. They are people who pervert grace. Their position is that the law is dead and they are under grace. The prescriptions of the law may apply to other people, but they no longer apply to them. They can do absolutely what they like. Grace is supreme; it can forgive any sin; the more the sin, the more the opportunities for grace to abound (*Romans* 6). The body is of no importance; what matters is the inward heart of man. All things belong to Christ, and, therefore, all things are theirs. And so for them there is nothing forbidden.

So Jude's heretics turn the grace of God into an excuse for flagrant immorality (verse 4); they even practise shameless unnatural vices, as the people of Sodom did (verse 7). They defile the flesh and think it no sin (verse 8). They allow their brute instincts to rule their lives (verse 10). With their sensual ways, they are like to make shipwreck of the love feasts of the church (verse 12). It is by their own lusts that they direct their lives (verse 16).

MODERN EXAMPLES OF THE ANCIENT HERESY

It is a curious and tragic fact of history that the church has never been entirely free of this antinomianism; and it is natural that it has flourished most in the ages when the wonder of grace was being rediscovered.

It appeared in the Ranters of the seventeenth century. The Ranters were pantheists and antinomians. A pantheist believes that God is everything; literally *all things* are Christ's, and Christ is the end of the law. They talked of "Christ within them," and paid no heed to the church or its ministry, and belittled scripture. One of them called Bottomley wrote: "It is not safe to go to the Bible to see what others have spoken and written of the mind of God as to see what God speaks within me, and to follow the doctrine and leading of it in me." When George Fox rebuked them for their lewd practices, they answered, "We are God." This may sound very fine, but, as John Wesley was to say, it most often resulted in "a gospel of the flesh." It was their argument that "swearing, adultery, drunkenness and theft are not sinful unless the person guilty of them apprehends them to be so." When Fox was a prisoner at Charing Cross they came to see him and mightily offended him by calling for drink and tobacco. They swore terribly and when Fox rebuked them, justified themselves by saying that Scripture tells us that Abraham, Jacob, Joseph, Moses, the priests, and the angel all swore. To which Fox replied that he who was before Abraham commanded, "Swear not at all." Richard Baxter said of them, "They conjoined a cursed doctrine of libertinism, which brought them to all abominable filthiness of life; they taught . . . that God regardeth not the actions of the outward man, but of the heart; and that to the pure all things are pure (even things forbidden) and so, as allowed by God, they spoke most hideous words of blasphemy, and many of them committed whoredoms commonly. . . . The horrid villainies of this sect did speedily extinguish it." Doubtless many of the Ranters were insane; doubtless some of them were pernicious and deliberate sensualists; but doubtless, too, some of them were earnest but misguided men, who had misunderstood the meaning of grace and freedom from the law.

Later John Wesley was to have trouble with the antinomians. He talks of them preaching a gospel of flesh and blood. At Jenninghall he says that "the antinomians had laboured hard in the Devil's service." At Birmingham he says that "the fierce, unclean, brutish, blasphemous antinomians" had utterly destroyed the spiritual life of the congregation. He tells of a certain Roger Ball who insinuated himself into the life of the congregation at Dublin. At first he seemed to be so spiritually-minded a man that the congregation welcomed him as being pre-eminently suited for the service and ministry of the church. He showed himself in time to be "full of guile and of the most abominable errors, one of which was that a believer had a right to all women." He would not communicate, for under grace a man must "touch not, taste not, handle not." He would not preach and abandoned the church services because, he said, "The dear Lamb is the only preacher."

Wesley, deliberately to show the position of these antinomians, related in his *Journal* a conversation which he had with one of them at Birmingham. It ran as follows. "Do you believe that you have nothing to do with the law of God?" "I have not; I am not under the law; I live by faith." "Have you, as living by faith, a right to everything in the world?" "I have. All is mine, since Christ is mine." "May you then take anything you will anywhere? Suppose out of a shop without the consent or knowledge of the owner?" "I may, if I want, for it is mine. Only I will not give offence." "Have you a right to all the women in the world?" "Yes, if they consent." "And is not that a sin?" "Yes, to him who thinks it is a sin; but not to those whose hearts are free."

Repeatedly Wesley had to meet these people, as George Fox

had to meet them. John Bunyan, too, came up against the Ranters who claimed complete freedom from the moral law and looked with contempt on the ethics of the stricter Christian. "These would condemn me as legal and dark, pretending that they only had attained perfection that could do what they would and not sin." One of them, whom Bunyan knew, "gave himself up to all manner of filthiness, especially uncleanness . . . and would laugh at all exhortations to sobriety. When I laboured to rebuke his wickedness, he would laugh the more."

Jude's heretics have existed in every Christian generation and, even if they do not go all the way, there are still many who in their heart of hearts trade upon God's forgiveness and make his grace an excuse to sin.

THE DENIAL OF GOD AND OF JESUS CHRIST

(ii) Of the antinomianism and blatant immorality of the heretics whom Jude condemns there is no doubt. The other two faults with which he charges them are not so obvious in their meaning. He charges them with, as the Revised Standard Version has it, "denying our only Master and Lord, Jesus Christ" (verse 4). The closing doxology is to "the only God," a phrase which occurs again in *Romans* 16: 27; 1 *Timothy* 1: 17; 1 *Timothy* 6: 15. The reiteration of the word *only* is significant. If Jude talks about our *only* Master and Lord and, about the *only* God, it is natural to assume that there must have been those who questioned the uniqueness of Jesus Christ and of God. Can we trace any such line of thought in the early church and, if so, does it fit in with any other evidence which hints within the letter itself may supply?

As so often in the New Testament, we are again in contact with that type of thought which came to be known as Gnosticism. Its basic idea was that this was a dualistic universe, a universe with two eternal principles in it. From the beginning of time there had always been spirit and matter. Spirit was essentially good; matter was essentially evil. Out of this flawed matter the world was created. Now God is pure spirit and, therefore, could not possibly handle this essentially evil matter. How then was creation effected? God put out a series of aeons or emanations; each of these aeons was farther away from him. At the end of this long chain, remote from God, there was an aeon who was able to touch matter; and it was this aeon, this distant and secondary god, who actually created the world.

Nor was this all that was in Gnostic thought. As the aeons in the series grew more distant from God, they grew more ignorant of him; and also grew more hostile to him. The creating aeon, at the end of the series, was at once totally ignorant of and totally hostile to God.

Having got that length, the Gnostics took another step. They identified the true God with the God of the New Testament and they identified the secondary, ignorant and hostile god with the God of the Old Testament. As they saw it, the God of creation was a different being from the God of revelation and redemption. Christianity on the other hand believes in the *only* God, the one God of creation, providence and redemption.

This was the Gnostic explanation of sin. It was because creation was carried out, in the first place, from evil matter and, in the second place, by an ignorant god, that sin and suffering and all imperfection existed.

This Gnostic line of thought had one curious, but perfectly logical, result. If the God of the Old Testament was ignorant of and hostile to the true God, it must follow that the people whom that ignorant God hurt were in fact *good* people. Clearly the hostile God would be hostile to the people who were the true servants of the true God. The Gnostics, therefore, so to speak, turned the Old Testament upside down and regarded its heroes as villains and its villains as heroes. So there was a sect of these Gnostics called Ophites, because they worshipped the serpent of Eden; and there were those who regarded Cain and Korah and Balaam as great heroes. It is these very people whom Jude uses as tragic and terrible examples of sin.

So we may take it that the heretics whom Jude attacks are Gnostics who denied the oneness of God, who regarded the God of creation as different from the God of redemption, who saw in the Old Testament God an ignorant enemy of the true God and who, therefore, turned the Old Testament upside down to regard its sinners as servants of the true God and its saints as servants of the hostile God.

Not only did these heretics deny the oneness of God, they also denied "our only Master and Lord Jesus Christ." That is to say, they denied the uniqueness of Jesus Christ. How does that fit in with the Gnostic ideas so far as they are known to us? We have seen that, according to Gnostic belief, God put out a series of aeons between himself and the world. The Gnostics regarded Jesus Christ as one of these aeons. They did not regard him as our *only* Master and Lord; he was only one among the many who were links between God and man, although he might be the highest and the closest of all.

There is still one other hint about these heretics in *Jude*, a hint which also fits in with what we know about the Gnostics. In verse 19 Jude describes them as "these who set up divisions." The heretics introduce some kind of class distinctions within the fellowship of the Church. What were these distinctions?

We have seen that between man and God there stretched an infinite series of aeons. The aim of man must be to achieve contact with God. To obtain this his soul must traverse this infinite series of links between God and man. The Gnostics held that to achieve this a very special and esoteric knowledge was required. So deep was this knowledge that only very few could attain to it.

The Gnostics, therefore, divided men into two classes, the *pneumatikoi* and the *psuchikoi*. The *pneuma* was the spirit of man, that which made him kin to God; and the *pneumatikoi* were the *spiritual* people, the people whose spirits were so highly developed and intellectual that they were able to climb the long ladder and reach God. These *pneumatikoi*, the

Gnostics claimed, were so spiritually and intellectually equipped that they could become as good as Jesus—Irenaeus says that some of them believed that the *pneumatikoi* could become *better* than Jesus and attain direct union with God.

On the other hand, the *psuchē* was simply the principle of physical life. All things which live had *psuchē*; it was something which man shared with the animal creation and even with growing plants. The *psuchikoi* were ordinary people; they had physical life but their *pneuma* was undeveloped and they were incapable of ever gaining the intellectual wisdom which would enable them to climb the long road to God. The *pneumatikoi* were a very small and select minority; the *psuchikoi* were the vast majority of ordinary people.

It is clear to see that this kind of belief was inevitably productive of spiritual snobbery and pride. It introduced into the church the worst kind of class distinction.

So, then, the heretics whom Jude attacks were men who denied the oneness of God and split him into an ignorant creating God and a truly spiritual God; who denied the uniqueness of Jesus Christ and saw him as only one of the links between God and man; who erected class distinctions within the church and limited fellowship with God to the intellectual few.

THE DENIAL OF THE ANGELS

(iii) It is further inferred that these heretics denied and insulted the angels. It is said they "reject authority, and revile the glorious ones" (verse 8). The words "authority" and "glorious ones" describe ranks in the Jewish hierarchy of angels. Verse 9 is a reference to a story in the *Assumption of Moses*. It is there told that Michael was given the task of burying the body of Moses. The devil tried to stop him and claim the body. Michael made no charge against the devil and said nothing against him. He said only, "The Lord rebuke you!" If Michael, the archangel, on such an occasion said nothing against the prince of evil angels, clearly no man can speak ill of the angels.

The Jewish belief in angels was very elaborate. Every nation had its protecting angel. Every person, even every child, had its angel. All the forces of nature, the wind and the sea and the fire and all the others, were under the control of angels. It could even be said "Every blade of grass has its angel." Clearly the heretics attacked the angels. It is likely that they said that the angels were the servants of the ignorant and hostile creator God and that a Christian must have nothing to do with them. We cannot quite be sure what lies behind this, but to all their other errors the heretics added the despising of the angels; and to Jude this seemed an evil thing.

JUDE AND THE NEW TESTAMENT

We must now examine the questions regarding the date and the authorship of *Jude*.

Jude had some difficulty in getting into the New Testament at all; it is one of the books whose position was always insecure and which were late in gaining full acceptance as part of the New Testament. Let us briefly set out the opinions of the great fathers and scholars of the early church about it.

Jude is included in the Muratorian Canon, which dates to about A.D. 170, and may be regarded as the first semi-official list of the books accepted by the Church. The inclusion of *Jude* is strange when we remember that the Muratorian Canon does not include in its list *Hebrews* and *First Peter*. But thereafter *Jude* is for long spoken of with a doubt. In the middle of the third century Origen knew and used it, but he was well aware that there were many who questioned its right to be scripture. Eusebius, the great scholar of the middle of the fourth century, made a deliberate examination of the position of the various books which were in use and he classes *Jude* amongst the books which are disputed.

Jerome, who produced the Vulgate, had his doubts about *Jude*; and it is in him that we find one of the reasons for the hesitation which was felt towards it. The strange thing about *Jude* is the way in which it quotes as authorities books which are *outside* the Old Testament. It uses as scripture certain books which were written between the Old and the New Testaments and were never generally regarded as scripture. Here are two definite instances. The reference in verse 9 to Michael disputing with the devil about the body of Moses is taken from an apocryphal book called *The Assumption of Moses*. In verses 14 and 15 Jude confirms his argument with a quotation from prophecy, as, indeed, is the habit of all the New Testament writers; but Jude's quotation is, in fact, taken from the *Book of Enoch*, which he appears to regard as scripture. Jerome tells us that it was Jude's habit of using non-scriptural books as scripture which made some people regard him with suspicion; and towards the end of the third century in Alexandria it was from the very same charge that Didymus defended him. It is perhaps the strangest thing in Jude that he uses these non-scriptural books as other New Testament writers use the prophets; and in verses 17 and 18 he makes use of a saying of the apostles which is not identifiable at all.

Jude, then, was one of the books which took a long time to gain an assured place in the New Testament; but by the fourth century its place was secure.

THE DATE

There are definite indications that *Jude* is not an early book. It speaks of the faith that was once delivered to the saints (verse 3). That way of speaking seems to look back a long way and to come from the time when there was a body of belief which was orthodoxy. In verses 17 and 18 he urges his people to remember the words of the apostles of the Lord Jesus Christ. That seems to come from a time when the apostles were no longer there and the Church was looking back on their teaching. The atmosphere of *Jude* is of a book which looks back.

Beside that we have to set the fact that, as it seems to us, *Second Peter* makes use of *Jude* to a very large extent. Anyone can see that its second chapter has the closest possible connection with *Jude*. It is quite certain that one of these writers was borrowing from the other. On general grounds it is much more likely that the author of *Second Peter* would incorporate the whole of *Jude* into his work than that *Jude* would, for no apparent reason, take over only one section of *Second Peter*. Now, if we believe that *Second Peter* uses it, *Jude* cannot be very late, even if it is not early.

It is true that *Jude* looks back on the apostles; but it is also true that, with the exception of John, all the apostles were dead by A.D. 70. Taking together the fact that *Jude* looks back on the apostles and the fact that *Second Peter* uses it, a date about A.D. 80 to 90 would suit the writing of *Jude*.

THE AUTHORSHIP OF JUDE

Who was this Jude, or Judas, who wrote this letter? He calls himself the servant of Jesus Christ and the brother of James. In the New Testament there are five people called Judas.

(i) There is the Judas of Damascus in whose house Paul was praying after his conversion on the Damascus road (*Acts* 9: 11).

(ii) There is Judas Barsabas, a leading figure in the councils of the church who, along with Silas, was the bearer to Antioch of the decision of the Council of Jerusalem when the door of the church was opened to the Gentiles (*Acts* 15: 22, 27, 32). This Judas was also a prophet (*Acts* 15: 32).

(iii) There is Judas Iscariot.

None of these three has ever seriously been considered as the author of this letter.

(iv) There is the second Judas in the apostolic band. John calls him Judas, not Iscariot (*John* 14: 22). In Luke's list of the Twelve there is an apostle whom the Authorized Version calls Judas *the brother* of James (*Luke* 6: 16; *Acts* 1: 13). If we were to depend solely on the Authorized Version we might well think that here we have a serious candidate for the authorship of his letter, and, indeed, Tertullian calls the writer the Apostle Judas. But in the Greek this man is simply called *Judas of James*. This is a very common idiom in Greek and almost always it means not *brother of*, but *son of*; so that *Judas of James* in the list of the Twelve is not Judas the *brother* of James but Judas the *son* of James, as all the newer translations show.

(v) There is the Judas who was the brother of Jesus (*Matthew* 13: 55; *Mark* 6: 3). If any of the New Testament Judases is the writer of this letter, it must be this one, for only he could truly be called *the brother of James*.

Is this little letter to be taken as a letter of the Judas who was the brother of our Lord? If so, it would give it a special interest. But there are objections.

(i) If Jude—to use the form of his name with which we are familiar—was the brother of Jesus, why does he not say so? Why does he identify himself as Jude the brother of James rather than as Jude the brother of Jesus? It would surely be explanation enough to say that he shrank from taking so great a title of honour to himself. Even if it was true that he was the brother of Jesus, he might well prefer in humility to call himself his servant, for Jesus was not only his brother but his Lord. Further, Jude the brother of James would in all probability never be outside Palestine in all his life. The church he would know would be that at Jerusalem, and of that church James was the undoubted head. If he was writing to churches in Palestine, his relationship to James was the natural thing to stress. When we come to think of it, it would be more surprising that Jude should call himself the brother of Jesus than that he should call himself the servant of Jesus Christ.

(ii) It is objected that Jude calls himself the servant of Jesus Christ and thereby calls himself an apostle. "Servants of God" was the Old Testament title for the prophets. God would not do anything without revealing it first to his servants the prophets (*Amos* 3: 7). What had been a prophetic title in the Old Testament became an apostolic title in the New Testament. Paul speaks of himself as the servant of Jesus Christ

(*Romans* 1: 1; *Philippians* 1: 1). He is spoken of as the servant of God in the Pastoral Epistles (*Titus* 1: 1), and that is also the title which James takes to himself (*James* 1: 1). It is concluded, therefore, that by calling himself "the Servant of Jesus Christ" Jude is claiming to be an apostle.

There are two answers to that. First, the title servant of Jesus Christ is not confined to the Twelve, for it is given by Paul to Timothy (*Philippians* 1: 1). Second, even if it is regarded as a title confined to the apostles in the wider sense of the word, we find the brethren of the Lord associated with the eleven after the Ascension (*Acts* 1: 14), and Jude, like James, may well have been among them; and we learn that the brothers of Jesus were prominent in the missionary work of the Church (1 *Corinthians* 9: 5). Such evidence as we have would tend to prove that Jude, the brother of our Lord, was one of the apostolic circle and that the title servant of Jesus Christ is perfectly applicable to him.

(iii) It is argued that the Jude of Palestine, who was the brother of Jesus, could not have written the Greek of this letter as he would be an Aramaic speaker. That is not a safe argument. Jude would certainly know Greek, for it was the *lingua franca* of the ancient world, which all men spoke in addition to their own language. The Greek of *Jude* is rugged and forceful; it might well be within Jude's competence to write it for himself and, even if he could not do so, he may well have had a helper and translator such as Peter had in Silvanus.

(iv) It might be argued that the heresy which Jude is attacking is Gnosticism and that Gnosticism is much more a Greek than a Jewish way of thought—and what would Jude of Palestine be doing writing to Greeks? But an odd fact about this heresy is that it is the very opposite of orthodox Judaism. The controller of all Jewish action was the sacred law; basic belief of Jewish religion was that there was one God; the Jewish belief in angels was highly developed. It is by no means difficult to suppose that when certain Jews entered the Christian faith, they swung to the other extreme. It is easy to imagine a Jew who had all his life been in servitude to the law suddenly discovering grace and plunging into antinomianism as a reaction against his former legalism; and reacting similarly against the traditional Jewish belief in one God and in angels. It is, in fact, easy to see in the heretics whom Jude attacks Jews who had come into the Christian Church rather as renegades from Judaism than as truly convinced Christians.

(v) Lastly, it might be argued that, if this letter had been known to have been the work of Jude the brother of Jesus, it would not have been so long in gaining an entry into the New Testament. But before the end of the first century the church was largely Gentile and the Jews were regarded as the enemies and the slanderers of the church. During his life-time Jesus's brothers had in fact been his enemies; and it could well have happened that a letter as Jewish as *Jude* might have had a struggle against prejudice to get into the New Testament, even if its author was the brother of Jesus.

JUDE THE BROTHER OF JESUS

If this letter is not the work of Jude, the brother of Jesus, what are the alternatives suggested? On the whole, they are two.

(i) The letter is the work of a man called Jude of whom nothing is otherwise known. This theory has to meet a twofold difficulty. First, there is the coincidence that this Jude is also the brother of James. Second, it is hard to explain how so small a letter ever came to have any authority at all, if it is the work of someone quite unknown.

(ii) The letter is pseudonymous. That is to say, it was written by someone else and then attached to the name of Jude. That was a common practice in the ancient world. Between the Old and New Testament scores of books were written and attached to the names of Moses, Enoch, Baruch, Isaiah, Solomon and many an other. No one saw anything wrong in that. But two things are to be noted about *Jude*.

(*a*) In all such publications the name to which the book was attached was a famous name; but Jude, the brother of our Lord, was a person who was completely obscure; he is not numbered amongst the great names of the early church. There is a story that in the days of Domitian there was a deliberate attempt to see to it that Christianity did not spread. News came to the Roman authority that certain descendants of Jesus were still alive, amongst them the grandsons of Jude. The Romans felt that it was possible that rebellion might gather around these men and they were ordered to appear before the Roman courts. When they did so, they were seen to be horny-handed sons of toil and were dismissed as being unimportant and quite harmless. Obviously Jude was Jude the obscure and there could have been no possible reason for attaching a book to the name of a man whom nobody knew.

(b) When a book was written pseudonymously, the reader was never left in any doubt as to the person whose name it was being attached to. If this letter had been issued as the work of Judas the brother of our Lord, he would certainly have been given that title in such a way that no one could mistake it; and yet, in fact, it is quite unclear who the author is.

Jude is obviously Jewish; its references and allusions are such that only a Jew could understand. It is simple and rugged; it is vivid and pictorial. It is clearly the work of a simple thinker rather than of a theologian. It fits Jude the brother of our Lord. It is attached to his name, and there could be no reason for so attaching it unless he did in fact write it.

It is our opinion that this little letter is actually the work of Judas, the brother of Jesus.

JUDE

WHAT IT MEANS TO BE A CHRISTIAN

Jude 1, 2

> Jude, the servant of Jesus Christ and the brother of James, sends this letter to the called who are beloved in God and kept by Jesus Christ. May mercy and peace and love be multiplied to you.

FEW things tell more about a man than the way in which he speaks of himself; few things are more revealing than the titles by which he wishes to be known. Jude calls himself the servant of Jesus Christ and the brother of James. At once this tells us two things about him.

(i) Jude was a man well content with the second place. He was not nearly so well known as James; and he is content to be known as the *brother of James*. In this he was the same as Andrew. Andrew is Simon Peter's brother (*John* 6: 8). He, too, was described by his relationship to a more famous brother. Jude and Andrew might well have been resentful of the brothers in whose shadow they had to live; but both had the great gift of gladly taking the second place.

(ii) The only title of honour which Jude would allow himself was *the servant of Jesus Christ*. The Greek is *doulos*, and it means more than *servant*, it means *slave*. That is to say, Jude regarded himself as having only one object and one distinction in life—to be for ever at the disposal of Jesus for service in his cause. The greatest glory which any Christian can attain is to be of use to Jesus Christ.

In this introduction Jude uses three words to describe Christians.

(i) Christians are those who are *called by God*. The Greek for *to call* is *kalein*; and *kalein* has three great areas of use. (*a*) It is the word for summoning a man *to office*, *to duty*, *and to responsibility*. The Christian is summoned to a task, to duty, to responsibility in the service of Christ. (*b*) It is the word for summoning a man to a *feast* or a *festival*. It is the

word for an invitation to a happy occasion. The Christian
is the man who is summoned to the joy of being the guest
of God. (*c*) It is the word for summoning a man to *judgment*.
It is the word for calling a man to court that he may give
account of himself. The Christian is in the end summoned
to appear before the judgment seat of Christ.

(ii) Christians are those who are *beloved in God*. It is this
great fact which determines the nature of the call. The call
to men is the call to be loved and to love. God calls men
to a task, but that task is an honour, not a burden. God
calls men to service, but it is the service of fellowship, not of
tyranny. In the end God calls men to judgment, but it is the
judgment of love as well as of justice.

(iii) Christians are those who are *kept by Christ*. The
Christian is never left alone; Christ is always the sentinel
of his life and the companion of his way.

THE CALL OF GOD

Jude 1, 2 (*continued*)

BEFORE we leave this opening passage, let us think a little
more about this calling of God and try to see something
of what it means.

(i) Paul speaks about being called to be an *apostle*
(*Romans* 1: 1; 1 *Corinthians* 1: 1). In Greek the word is
apostolos; it comes from the verb *apostellein*, *to send out*, and
an apostle is therefore, *one who is sent out*. That is to say,
the Christian is the ambassador of Christ. He is sent out
into the world to speak for Christ, to act for Christ, to live
for Christ. By his life he commends, or fails to commend,
Christ to others.

(ii) Paul speaks about being called to be *saints* (*Romans*
1: 7; 1 *Corinthians* 1: 2). The word for *saint* is *hagios*, which
is also very commonly translated *holy*. Its root idea is
difference. The Sabbath is holy because it is different from

other days; God is supremely holy because he is different
from men. To be called to be a *saint* is to be called to
be *different*. The world has its own standards and its own
scale of values. The difference for the Christian is that Christ
is the only standard and loyalty to Christ the only value.

(iii) The Christian is called *according to the purpose of God*
(*Romans* 8: 28). God's call goes out to every man, although
every man does not accept it; and this means that for every
man God has a purpose. The Christian is the man who
submits himself to the purpose God has for him.

Paul has much to say about this calling of God, and we
can set it down only very summarily. It sets before a man a
great hope (*Ephesians* 1: 18; 4: 4). It should be a unifying
influence binding men together by the conviction that they all
have a part in the purpose of God (*Ephesians* 4: 4). It is
an *upward* calling (*Philippians* 3: 14), setting a man's feet on
the way to the stars. It is a *heavenly* calling (*Hebrews* 3: 1),
making a man think of the things which are invisible and
eternal. It is a *holy* calling, a call to consecration to God.
It is a calling which covers a man's ordinary every-day task
(1 *Corinthians* 7: 20). It is a calling which does not alter
because God does not change his mind (*Romans* 11: 29).
It knows no human distinctions and cuts across the world's
classifications and scale of importances (1 *Corinthians* 1: 26).
It is something of which the Christian must be worthy
(*Ephesians* 4: 1; 2 *Thessalonians* 1: 11); and all life must be
one long effort to make it secure (2 *Peter* 1: 10).

The calling of God is the privilege, the challenge and the
inspiration of the Christian life.

DEFENDING THE FAITH

Jude 3

Beloved, when I was in the midst of devoting all my energy to
writing to you about the faith which we all share, I felt that I was
compelled to write a letter to you to urge you to engage upon the
struggle to defend the faith which was once and for all delivered to
God's consecrated people.

HERE we have the occasion of the letter. Jude had been engaged on writing a treatise about the Christian faith; but there had come news that evil and misguided men had been spreading destructive teaching. The conviction had come to him that he must lay aside his treatise and write this letter.

Jude fully realized his duty to be the watchman of the flock of God. The purity of their faith was threatened and he rushed to defend both them and the faith. That involved setting aside the work on which he had been engaged; but often it is much better to write a tract for the times than a treatise for the future. It may be that Jude never again got the chance to write the treatise he had planned; but the fact is that he did more for the church by writing this urgent little letter than he could possibly have done by leaving a long treatise on the faith.

In this passage there are certain truths about the faith which we hold.

(i) The faith is *something which is delivered to us*. The facts of the Christian faith are not something which we have discovered for ourselves. In the true sense of the word they are *tradition*, something which has been handed down from generation to generation until it has come to us. They go back in an unbroken chain to Jesus Christ himself.

There is something to be added to that. The facts of the faith are indeed something which we have not discovered for ourselves. It is, therefore, true that the Christian tradition is not something handed down in the cold print of books; it is something which is passed on from person to person through the generations. The chain of Christian tradition is a living chain whose links are men and women who have experienced the wonder of the facts.

(ii) The Christian faith is *something which is once and for all delivered to us*. There is in it an unchangeable quality. That is not to say that each age has not to rediscover the Christian faith; but it does say that there is an unchanging nucleus in it—and the permanent centre of it is that Jesus Christ came into the world and lived and died to bring salvation to men.

(iii) The Christian faith is *something which is entrusted to God's consecrated people*. That is to say, the Christian faith is not the possession of any one person but of the church. It comes down within the church, it is preserved within the church, and it is understood within the church.

(iv) The Christian faith is *something which must be defended*. Every Christian must be its defender. If the Christian tradition comes down from generation to generation, each generation must hand it on uncorrupted and unperverted. There are times when that is difficult. The word Jude uses for to *defend* is *epagōnizesthai*, which contains the root of our English word *agony*. The defence of the faith may well be a costly thing; but that defence is a duty which falls on every generation of the Church.

THE PERIL FROM WITHIN

Jude 4

For certain men have wormed their way into the Church—long before this they were designated for judgment—impious creatures they are—who twist the grace of God into a justification of blatant immorality and who deny our only Master and Lord, Jesus Christ.

HERE is the peril which made Jude lay aside the treatise he was about to write and take up his pen to write this burning letter. The peril came *from within the church*.

Certain men, as the Authorized Version has it, had *crept in unawares*. The Greek (*pareisduein*) is a very expressive word. It is used of the spacious and seductive words of a clever pleader seeping gradually into the minds of a judge and jury; it is used of an outlaw slipping secretly back into the country from which he has been expelled; it is used of the slow and subtle entry of innovations into the life of state, which in the end undermine and break down the ancestral laws. It always indicates a stealthy insinuation of something evil into a society or situation.

Certain evil men had insinuated themselves into the church. They were the kind of men for whom judgment was waiting. They were impious creatures, godless in their thought and life. Jude picks out two characteristics about them.

(i) They perverted the grace of God into an excuse for blatant immorality. The Greek which we have translated *blatant immorality* is a grim and terrible word (*aselgeia*). The corresponding adjective is *aselgēs*. Most men try to hide their sin; they have enough respect for common decency not to wish to be found out. But the *aselgēs* is the man who is so lost to decency that he does not care who sees his sin. It is not that he arrogantly and proudly flaunts it; it is simply that he can publicly do the most shameless things, because he has ceased to care for decency at all.

These men were undoubtedly tinged with Gnosticism and its belief that, since the grace of God was wide enough to cover any sin, a man could sin as he liked. The more he sinned, the greater the grace, therefore, why worry about sin? Grace was being perverted into a justification for sin.

(ii) They denied our only Lord and Master, Jesus Christ. There is more than one way in which a man can deny Jesus Christ. (*a*) He can deny him in the day of persecution. (*b*) He can deny him for the sake of convenience. (*c*) He can deny him by his life and conduct. (*d*) He can deny him by developing false ideas about him.

If these men were Gnostics, they would have two mistaken ideas about Jesus. First, since the body, being matter, was evil, they would hold that Jesus only *seemed* to have a body and was a kind of spirit ghost in the apparent shape of a man. The Greek for *to seem* is *dokein*; and these men were called *Docetists*. They would deny the real manhood of Jesus Christ. Second, they would deny his uniqueness. They believed that there were many stages between the evil matter of this world and the perfect spirit which is God; and they believed that Jesus was only one of the many stages on the way.

No wonder Jude was alarmed. He was faced with a situation in which there had wormed their way into the church men who were twisting the grace of God into a justification, and even a reason, for sinning in the most blatant way; and who denied both the manhood and the uniqueness of Jesus Christ.

THE DREADFUL EXAMPLES

Jude 5–7

It is my purpose to remind you—although you already possess full and final knowledge of all that matters—that, after the Lord had brought the people out of Egypt in safety, he subsequently destroyed those who were unbelieving; and that he has placed under guard in eternal chains in the abyss of darkness, to await the judgment which shall take place on the great day, the angels who did not keep their own rank but left their own proper habitation. Just so Sodom and Gomorrah and the surrounding cities, who in the same way as these took their fill of sexual sin and strayed after perverted sexual immorality, are a warning by the way in which they paid the penalty of eternal fire.

1. THE FATE OF ISRAEL

JUDE issues a warning to the evil men who were perverting the belief and conduct of the church. He tells them that he is, in fact, doing nothing other than remind them of things of which they are perfectly well aware. In a sense it is true to say that all preaching within the Christian church is not so much bringing to men new truth as confronting them with truth they already know, but have forgotten or are disregarding.

To understand the first two examples which Jude cites from history we must understand one thing. The evil men who were corrupting the church did not regard themselves as enemies of the church and of Christianity; they regarded themselves as the advanced thinkers, a cut above the ordinary Christian, the spiritual élite. Jude chooses his examples to make clear that, even if a man has received the greatest privileges, he may still fall away into disaster, and even those who have received the greatest privileges from God cannot consider themselves safe but must be on constant watch against the mistaken things.

The first example is from the history of Israel. He goes for his story to *Numbers* 13 and 14. The mighty hand of God had delivered the people from slavery in Egypt. What greater act of deliverance could there be than that? The guidance of God had brought the people safely across the desert to the borders of the Promised Land. What greater demonstration of his Providence could there be than that? So, at the very borders of the Promised Land, at Kadesh-barnea, spies were sent out to spy out the land before the final invasion took place. With the exception of Caleb and Joshua, the spies came back with the opinion that the dangers ahead were so terrible and the people so strong, that they could never win their way into the Promised Land. The people rejected the report of Caleb and Joshua, who were for going on, and accepted the report of those who insisted that the case was hopeless. This was a clear act of disobedience to God and of complete lack of faith in him. The consequence was that God gave sentence that of these people, with the exception of Joshua and Caleb, all over twenty would never enter the Promised Land but would wander in the wilderness until they were dead (*Numbers* 14: 32, 33; 32: 10–13).

This was a picture which haunted the mind of both Paul and the writer to the Hebrews (1 *Corinthians* 10: 5–11; *Hebrews* 3: 18—4: 2). It is the proof that even the man with the greatest privilege can meet with disaster before the end, if he falls away from obedience and lapses from faith. Johnstone Jeffrey tells of a great man who absolutely refused to have his life-story written before his death. "I have seen," he said, "too many men fall out on the last lap." John Wesley warned, "Let, therefore, none presume on past mercies, as if they were out of danger." In his dream John Bunyan saw that even from the gates of heaven there was a way to hell.

Jude warns these men that, great as their privileges have

been, they must still have a care lest disaster come upon
them. It is a warning which each of us would do well to heed.

THE DREADFUL EXAMPLES

2. THE FATE OF THE ANGELS

Jude 5–7 (continued)

THE second dreadful example which Jude takes is the fallen
angels.

The Jews had a very highly developed doctrine of angels,
the servants of God. In particular the Jews believed that
every nation had its presiding angel. In the *Septuagint*, the
Greek version of the Hebrew Scriptures, *Deuteronomy* 32: 8
reads, "When the Most High divided the nations, when he
separated the sons of Adam, he set the bounds of the nations
according to the number of the angels of God." That is to
say, to each nation there was an angel.

The Jews believed in a fall of the angels and much is said
about this in the *Book of Enoch* which is so often behind
the thought of Jude. In regard to this there were two lines
of tradition.

(i) The first saw the fall of the angels as due to pride
and rebelliousness. That legend gathered especially round the
name of Lucifer, the light-bringer, the son of the morning.
As the Authorized Version has it, Isaiah writes, "How art
thou fallen from heaven, O Lucifer, son of the morning!"
(*Isaiah* 14: 12). When the seventy returned from their mission
and told Jesus of their successes, he warned them against
pride, "I saw Satan fall like lightning from heaven" (*Luke*
10: 18). The idea was that there was civil war in heaven.
The angels rose against God and were cast out; and Lucifer
was the leader of the rebellion.

(ii) The second stream of tradition finds its scriptural echo
in *Genesis* 6: 1–4. In this line of thought the angels, attracted
by the beauty of mortal women, left heaven to seduce them
and so sinned.

In the first case the fall of the angels was due to *pride*; in the second case it was due to *lust* for forbidden things.

In effect Jude takes the two ideas and puts them together. He says that the angels left their own rank; that is to say, they aimed at an office which was not for them. He also says that they left their own proper habitation; that is to say, they came to earth to live with the daughters of men.

All this seems strange to us; it moves in a world of thought and traditions from which we have moved away.

But Jude's warning is clear. Two things brought ruin to the angels—pride and lust. Even although they were angels and heaven had been their dwelling-place, they none the less sinned and for their sin were reserved for judgment. To those reading Jude's words for the first time the whole line of thought was plain, for *Enoch* had much to say about the fate of these fallen angels. So Jude was speaking to his people in terms that they could well understand and telling them that, if pride and lust ruined the angels in spite of all their privileges, pride and lust could ruin them. The evil men within the church were proud enough to think that they knew better than the church's teaching and lustful enough to pervert the grace of God into a justification for blatant immorality. Whatever be the ancient background of his words, Jude's warning is still valid. The pride which knows better than God and the desire for forbidden things are the way to ruin in time and in eternity.

THE DREADFUL EXAMPLES

3. SODOM AND GOMORRAH

Jude 5–7 (continued)

THE third example Jude chose is the destruction of Sodom and Gomorrah. Notorious for their sins, these cities were obliterated by the fire of God. Sir George Adam Smith in *The Historical Geography of the Holy Land* points out that no

incident in history ever made such an impression on the
Jewish people, and that Sodom and Gomorrah are time and
time again used in Scripture as the examples *par excellence*
of the sin of man and the judgment of God; they are so used
even by Jesus himself (*Deuteronomy* 29: 23; 32: 32; *Amos*
4: 11; *Isaiah* 1: 9; 3: 9; 13: 19; *Jeremiah* 23: 14; 49: 18;
50: 40; *Zephaniah* 2: 9; *Lamentations* 4: 6; *Ezekiel* 16: 46, 49,
53, 55; *Matthew* 10: 15; 11: 24; *Luke* 10: 12; 17: 29; *Romans*
9: 29; 2 *Peter* 2: 6; *Revelation* 11: 8). "The glare of Sodom
and Gomorrah is flung down the whole length of Scripture
history."

The story of the final wickedness of Sodom and Gomorrah
is told in *Genesis* 19: 1–11, and the tragic tale of their destruction in the passage immediately following (*Genesis*
19: 12–28). The sin of Sodom is one of the most horrible
stories in history. Ryle has called it a "repulsive incident."
The real horror of the incident is cloaked a little in the
Authorized and Revised Versions by a Hebrew turn of speech.
Two angelic visitors had come to Lot. At his pressing invitation they came into his house to be his guests. When
they were there, the inhabitants of Sodom surrounded the
house, demanding that Lot should bring out his visitors that
they should *know* them. In Hebrew *to know* is the word for
sexual intercourse. It is said, for instance, that Adam *knew*
his wife, and she conceived, and bore Cain (*Genesis* 4: 1).
What the men of Sodom were bent on was homosexual intercourse with Lot's two visitors—sodomy, the word in which
their sin is commemorated.

It was after this that Sodom and Gomorrah were obliterated
from the face of the earth. The neighbouring cities were
Zoar, Admah and Zeboim (*Deuteronomy* 29: 23; *Hosea* 11: 8).
This disaster was localized in the dreadful desert in the region
of the Dead Sea, a region which Sir George Adam Smith
calls, "This awful hollow, this bit of the infernal regions
come to the surface, this hell with the sun shining into it."
It was there that the cities were said to have been; and it
was said that under that scorched and barren earth there still

smouldered an eternal fire of destruction. The soil is
bituminous with oil below, and Sir George Adam Smith con-
jectures that what happened was this: "In this bituminous
soil took place one of these terrible explosions and con-
flagrations which have broken out in the similar geology of
North America. In such soil reservoirs of oil and gas are
formed, and suddenly discharged by their own pressure or by
earthquake. The gas explodes, carrying high into the air
masses of oil which fall back in fiery rain, and are so in-
extinguishable that they float afire on water." It was by such
an eruption of fire that Sodom and Gomorrah were destroyed.
That awful desert was only a day's journey from Jerusalem
and men never forgot this divine judgment on sin.

So, then, Jude reminds these evil men of the fate of those
who in ancient times defied the moral law of God. It is
reasonable to suppose that those whom Jude attacks had also
descended to sodomy and that they were perverting the grace
of God to cover even this.

Jude is insisting that they should remember that sin and
judgment go hand in hand, and that they should repent in time

CONTEMPT FOR THE ANGELS

Jude 8, 9

> In the same way these, too, with their dreams, defile the flesh, and
> set at naught the celestial powers, and speak evil of the angelic
> glories. When the archangel Michael himself was disputing with the
> devil about the body of Moses, he did not venture to launch against
> him an evil-speaking accusation, but said, "The Lord rebuke you!"

JUDE begins this passage by comparing the evil men with the
false prophets whom Scripture condemns. *Deuteronomy* 13:
1–5 sets down what is to be done with "the prophet or
the dreamer of dreams" who corrupts the nations and seduces
the people from their loyalty to God. Such a prophet is
to be mercilessly killed. These men whom Jude attacks are

false prophets, dreamers of false dreams, seducers of the people, and must be treated as such. Their false teaching issued in two things.

(i) It made them defile the flesh. We have already seen the twofold direction of their teaching on the flesh. First, the flesh was entirely evil, and, therefore, of no importance; and so the instincts of the body could be given their way without control. Second, the grace of God was all-forgiving and all-sufficient and therefore, sin did not matter since grace would forgive every sin. Sin was only the means whereby grace was given its opportunity to operate.

(ii) They despised angels. Celestial powers and angelic glories are names for ranks of angels within the angelic hierarchy. This follows immediately after the citing of Sodom and Gomorrah as dreadful examples; and part of the sin of Sodom was the desire of its people to misuse its angelic visitors (*Genesis* 19: 1–11). The men Jude attacks spoke evil of the angels. To prove how terrible a thing that was Jude cites an instance from an apocryphal book, *The Assumption of Moses*. One of the strange things about Jude is that he so often makes his quotations from these apocryphal books. Such quotations seem strange to us; but these books were very widely used at the time when Jude was writing and the quotations would be very effective.

The story in *The Assumption of Moses* runs as follows. The strange story of the death of Moses is told in *Deuteronomy* 34: 1–6. *The Assumption of Moses* goes on to add the further story that the task of burying the body of Moses was given to the archangel Michael. The devil disputed with Michael for possession of the body. He based his claim on two grounds. Moses's body was matter; matter was evil; and, therefore, the body belonged to him, for matter was his domain. Second, Moses was a murderer, for had not he slain the Egyptian whom he saw smiting the Hebrew (*Exodus* 2: 11, 12). And, if he was a murderer, the devil had a claim on his body. The point Jude is making is this. Michael was engaged on a task given him by God; the devil was seeking to stop him and was making claims he had no right to make. But even in a collection of circumstances like that Michael spoke no evil of the devil but simply said, "The Lord rebuke you!" If the greatest of the good angels refused to speak evil of the greatest of the evil angels, even in circumstances like that, surely no human being may speak evil of any angel.

What the men Jude is attacking were saying about the angels we do not know. Perhaps they were saying that they did not exist; perhaps they were saying they were evil. This passage means very little to us, but no doubt it would be a weighty rebuke to those to whom Jude addressed it.

THE GOSPEL OF THE FLESH

Jude 10

> But these people speak evil of everything which they do not under-
> stand, whereas they allow themselves to be corrupted by the
> knowledge which their instincts give them, living at the mercy of
> their instincts, like beasts without reason.

JUDE says two things about the evil men whom he is attacking.

(i) They criticize everything which they do not understand. Anything which is out of their orbit and their experience they disregard as worthless and irrelevant. "Spiritual things are spiritually discerned" (1 *Corinthians* 2: 14). They have no spiritual discernment, and, therefore, they are blind to, and contemptuous of, all spiritual realities.

(ii) They allow themselves to be corrupted by the things they do understand. What they do understand are the fleshly instincts which they share with the brute beasts. Their way of life is to allow these instincts to have their way; their values are fleshly values. Jude describes men who have lost all awareness of spiritual things and for whom the things de-manded by the animal instincts are the only standards.

The terrible thing is that the first condition is the direct result of the second. The tragedy is that no man is born without a sense of the spiritual things but can lose that sense until for him the spiritual things cease to exist. A man may lose any faculty, if he refuses to use it. We discover that with such simple things as games and skills. If we give up playing a game, we lose the ability to play it. If we give up practising a skill—such as playing the piano—we lose it. We discover that in such things as abilities. We may know something of a foreign language, but if we never speak or read it, we lose it. Every man can hear the voice of God; and every man has the animal instincts on which, indeed, the future existence of the race depends. But, if he consistently refuses to listen to God and makes his instincts the sole dynamic of his conduct, in the end he will be unable to hear the voice of God and will have nothing left to be his master but his brute desires. It is a terrible thing for a man to reach a stage where he is deaf to God and blind to goodness; and that is the stage which the men whom Jude attacks had reached.

LESSONS FROM HISTORY

Jude 11

> Woe to them because they walk in the way of Cain; they fling themselves into the error of Balaam; they perish in Korah's opposition to God.

JUDE now goes to Hebrew history for parallels to the wicked men of his own day; and from it he draws the examples of three notorious sinners.

(i) First, there is Cain, the murderer of his brother Abel (*Genesis* 4: 1–15). In Hebrew tradition Cain stood for two things. (*a*) He was the first murderer in the world's history; and, as *The Wisdom of Solomon* has it, "he himself perished in the fury wherewith he murdered his brother" (*Wisdom* 10: 3). It may well be that Jude is implying that those who delude others are nothing other than murderers of the souls of men and, therefore, the spiritual descendants of Cain. (*b*) But in Hebrew tradition Cain came to stand for something more than that. In Philo he stands for selfishness. In the Rabbinic teaching he is the type of the cynical man. In the Jerusalem *Targum* he is depicted as saying: "There is neither judgment nor judge; there is no other world; no good reward will be given to the good and no vengeance taken on the wicked; nor is there any pity in the creation or the government of the world." To the Hebrew thinkers Cain was the cynical, materialistic unbeliever who believed neither in God nor in the moral order of the world and who, therefore, did exactly as he liked. So Jude is charging his opponents with defying God and denying the moral order of the world. It remains true that the man who chooses to sin has still to reckon with God and to learn, always with pain and sometimes with tragedy, that no man can defy the moral order of the world with impunity.

(ii) Second, there is Balaam. In Old Testament thought, in Jewish teaching and even in the New Testament (*Revelation* 2: 14) Balaam is the great example of those who taught Israel to sin. In the Old Testament there are two stories about him. One is quite clear, and very vivid and dramatic. The other is more shadowy, but much more terrible; and it is it which left its mark on Hebrew thought and teaching.

The first is in *Numbers* chapter 22 to 24. There it is told how Balak attempted to persuade Balaam to curse the people of Israel, for he feared their power, five times offering him large rewards. Balaam refused to be persuaded by Balak, but his covetousness stands out and it is clear that only the fear of what God would do to him kept him from striking a dreadful bargain. Balaam already emerges as a detestable character.

In *Numbers* 25 there is the second story. Israel is seduced into the worship of Baal with dreadful and repulsive moral consequences. As we read later (*Numbers* 31: 8, 16), it was Balaam who was responsible for that seduction, and he perished miserably because he taught others to sin.

Out of this composite story Balaam stands for two things. (*a*) He stands for the covetous man who was prepared to sin in order to gain reward. (*b*) He stands for the evil man who was guilty of the greatest of all sins—that of teaching others to sin. So Jude is declaring of the wicked men of his own day that they are ready to leave the way of righteousness to make gain; and that they are teaching others to sin. To sin for the sake of gain is bad; but to teach another to sin is the worst of all.

(iii) Third, there was Korah. His story is in *Numbers* 16: 1–35. The sin of Korah was that he rebelled against the guidance of Moses when the sons of Aaron and the tribe of Levi were made the priests of the nation. That was a decision which Korah was not willing to accept; he wished to exercise a function which he had no right to exercise; and when he did so he perished terribly and all his companions in wickedness with him. Korah stands for the man who refuses to accept authority and reaches out for things which he has no right to have. So Jude is charging his opponents with defying the legitimate authority of the church, and of, therefore, preferring their own way to the way of God. We should remember that if we take certain things which pride incites us to take, the consequences can be disastrous.

THE PICTURE OF WICKED MEN

Jude 12–16

These people are hidden rocks which threaten to wreck your Love Feasts. These are the people who at your feasts revel with their own cliques without a qualm. They have no feeling of responsibility to anyone except themselves. They are clouds which drop no water but are blown past by the wind. They are fruitless trees in autumn's harvest time, twice dead and torn up by the roots. They are wild sea waves, frothing out their own shameless deeds. They

are wandering stars and the abyss of darkness has been prepared
for them for ever. It was of these, too, that Enoch, who was the
seventh from Adam, prophesied when he said:

> Behold the Lord has come with ten thousands of his holy
> ones, to execute judgment upon all and to convict all the impious
> for all the deeds of their impiousness, which they have impiously
> committed, and for the harsh things which impious sinners
> have said against him.

For these people are grumblers. They querulously complain against
the part in life which God has allotted to them. Their conduct is
governed by their desires. Their mouths speak swelling words. They
toady to men for what they can get out of it.

THIS is one of the great passages of invective of the New
Testament. It is blazing moral indignation at its hottest. As
Moffatt puts it: "Sky, land and sea are ransacked for illustrations of the character of these men." Here is a series of
vivid pictures, every one with significance. Let us take them
one by one.

(i) They are like hidden rocks which threaten to wreck the
Love Feasts of the Church. This is the one case in which
there is doubt about what Jude is actually saying but of one
thing there is no doubt—the evil men were a peril to the
Love Feasts. The Love Feast, the *Agapē*, was one of the earliest
features of the Church. It was a meal of fellowship held on
the Lord's Day. To it everyone brought what he could, and
all shared alike. It was a lovely idea that the Christians in
each little house church should sit down on the Lord's Day
to eat in fellowship together. No doubt there were some who
could bring much and others who could bring only little.
For many of the slaves it was perhaps the only decent meal
they ever ate.

But very soon the *Agapē* began to go wrong. We can see
it going wrong in the church at Corinth, when Paul declares
that at the Corinthian Love Feasts there is nothing but
division. They are divided into cliques and sections; some
have too much, and others starve; and the meal for some
has become a drunken revel (1 *Corinthians* 11: 17–22). Unless

the *Agapē* was a true fellowship, it was a travesty, and very soon it had begun to belie its name.

Jude's opponents were making a travesty of the Love Feasts. The Revised Standard Version says that he calls them "blemishes on your love feasts" (verse 12); and that agrees with the parallel passage in *Second Peter*—"blots and blemishes" (2 *Peter* 2: 13). We have translated Jude's expression "hidden rocks."

The difficulty is that Peter and Jude do not use the same word, although they use words which are very similar. The word in *Second Peter* is *spilos*, which unquestionably means a *blot* or *spot*; but the word in Jude is *spilas*, which is very rare. Just possibly it may mean a *blot*, because in later Greek it could be used for the spots and markings on an opal stone. But in ordinary Greek by far its most common meaning was *a submerged*, or *half-submerged, rock on which a ship could be easily ship-wrecked*. We think that here the second meaning is much more likely.

In the Love Feast people were very close together in heart and there was the kiss of peace. These wicked men were using the Love Feasts as a cloak under which to gratify their lusts. It is a dreadful thing, if men enter into the church and use the opportunities which its fellowship gives for their own perverted ends. These men were like sunken rocks on which the fellowship of the Love Feasts was in danger of being wrecked.

THE SELFISHNESS OF WICKED MEN

Jude 12–16 (*continued*)

(ii) These wicked men revel in their own cliques and have no feeling of responsibility for anyone except themselves. These two things go together for they both stress their essential selfishness.

(*a*) They revel in their own cliques without a qualm. This

is exactly the situation which Paul condemns in *First Corinthians*. The Love Feast was supposed to be an act of fellowship; and the fellowship was demonstrated by the sharing of all things. Instead of sharing, the wicked men kept to their own clique and kept to themselves all they had. In *First Corinthians* Paul actually goes the length of saying that the Love Feast could become a drunken revel in which every man grabbed at all that he could get (1 *Corinthians* 11: 21). No man can ever claim to know what church membership means, if in the church he is out for what he can get and remains within his own little group.

(*b*) We have translated the next phrase: "They have no feeling of responsibility for anyone except themselves." The Greek literally means "shepherding themselves." The duty of a leader of the Church is to be a shepherd of the flock of God (*Acts* 20: 28). The false shepherd cared far more for himself than for the sheep which were supposed to be within his care. Ezekiel describes the false shepherds from whom their privileges were to be taken away: "As I live, says the Lord God, because my sheep have become a prey and my sheep have become food for all the wild beasts, since there was no shepherd; and because my shepherds have not searched for my sheep, but the shepherds have fed themselves, and have not fed my sheep. . . . Behold I am against the shepherds; and I will require my sheep at their hand, and put a stop to their feeding the sheep" (*Ezekiel* 34: 8–10). The man who feels no responsibility for the welfare of anyone except himself stands condemned.

So, then, Jude condemns the selfishness which destroys fellowship and the lack of the sense of responsibility for others.

(iii) The wicked men are like clouds blown past by the wind, which drop no rain and like trees in harvest time which have no fruit. These two phrases go together, for they describe people who make great claims but are essentially useless. There were times in Palestine when people would pray for rain. At such a time a cloud might pass across the sky, bringing with it the promise of rain. But there were times when the promise was only an illusion, the cloud was blown on and the rain never came. In any harvest time there were trees which looked as if they were heavy with fruit but which, when men came to gather from them, gave no fruit at all.

At the heart of this lies a great truth. Promise without performance is useless and in the New Testament nothing is so unsparingly condemned as uselessness No amount of outward show or fine words will take the place of usefulness to others. As it has been put: "If a man is not good for something, he is good for nothing."

THE FATE OF DISOBEDIENCE

Jude 12–16 (*continued*)

JUDE goes on to use a vivid picture of these evil men. "They are like wild sea waves frothing out their own shameless deeds." The picture is this. After a storm, when the waves have been lashing the shore with their frothing spray and their spume, there is always left on the shore a fringe of seaweed and driftwood and all kinds of unsightly litter from the sea. That is always an unlovely scene. But in the case of one sea it is grimmer than in any other. The waters of the Dead Sea can be whipped up into waves, and these waves, too, cast up driftwood on the shore; but in this instance there is a unique circumstance. The waters of the Dead Sea are so impregnated with salt that they strip the bark of any driftwood in them; and, when such wood is cast up on the shore, it gleams bleak and white, more like dried bones than wood. The deeds of the wicked men are like the useless and unsightly litter which the waves leave scattered on the beach after a storm and resemble the skeleton-like relics of Dead Sea storms. The picture vividly portrays the ugliness of the deeds of Jude's opponents.

Jude uses still another picture. The wicked men are like the wandering stars that are kept in the abyss of darkness for their disobedience. This is a picture directly taken from the *Book of Enoch*. In that book the stars and the angels are sometimes identified; and there is a picture of the fate of the stars who, disobedient to God, left their appointed orbit and were destroyed. In his journey through the earth Enoch came to a place where he saw, "neither a heaven above nor a firmly founded earth, but a place chaotic and horrible." He goes on: "And there I saw seven stars of the heaven bound together in it, like great mountains and burning with fire. Then I said, 'For what sin are they bound, and on account of what have they been cast in hither?' Then said Uriel, one of the holy angels, who was with me and who was chief over them, 'Enoch, why dost thou ask and why art thou eager for the truth? These are the numbers of the stars of heaven which have transgressed the commandment of the Lord, and are bound here till ten thousand years, the time entailed by their sins, are consummated'" (*Enoch* 21: 1–6). The fate of the wandering stars is typical of the fate of the man who disobeys God's commandments and, as it were, takes his own way.

Jude then confirms all this with a prophecy; but the prophecy is again taken from *Enoch*. The actual passage runs: "And behold! He cometh with ten thousands of his holy ones to execute judgment upon all, and to destroy all the ungodly; and to convict all flesh of all the works of their ungodliness which they have ungodly committed, and of all the hard things which ungodly sinners have spoken against him" (*Enoch* 1: 9).

This quotation has raised many questions in regard to *Jude* and *Enoch*. There is no doubt that in the days of Jude, and in the days of Jesus, *Enoch* was a very popular book which every pious Jew would know and read. Ordinarily, when the New Testament writers wish to confirm their words, they do so with a quotation from the Old Testament, using it as the word of God. Are we then to regard *Enoch* as sacred Scripture, since Jude uses it exactly as he would have used one of the prophets? Or, are we to take the view of which Jerome speaks, and say that *Jude* cannot be Scripture, because it makes the mistake of using as Scripture a book which is, in fact, not Scripture?

We need waste no time upon this debate. The fact is that Jude, a pious Jew, knew and loved the *Book of Enoch* and had grown up in a circle where it was regarded with respect and even reverence; and he takes his quotation from it perfectly naturally, knowing that his readers would recognize it, and respect it. He is simply doing what all the New Testament writers do, as every writer must in every age, and speaking to men in language which they will recognize and understand.

THE CHARACTERISTICS OF EVIL MEN

Jude 12–16 (*continued*)

IN verse 16 Jude sets down three last characteristics of the evil men.

(i) They are grumblers, for ever discontented with the life which God has allotted to them. In this picture he uses two words, one which was very familiar to his Jewish readers and one which was very familiar to his Greek readers.

(*a*) The first is *goggustēs*. (*Gg* in Greek is pronounced *ng*). The word describes the discontented voices of the murmurers and is the same as is so often used in the Greek Old Testament for the *murmurings* of the children of Israel against Moses as he led them through the wilderness (*Exodus* 15: 24; 17: 3; *Numbers* 14: 29). Its very sound describes the low mutter of resentful discontent which rose from the rebellious people. These wicked men in the time of Jude are the modern counterparts of the murmuring children of Israel in the desert, people full of sullen complaints against the guiding hand of God.

(*b*) The second is *mempsimoiros*. It is made up of two Greek words, *memphesthai*, which means *to blame* and *moira*, which means *one's allotted fate or life*. A *mempsimoiros* was a man who was for ever grumbling about life in general. Theophrastus was the great master of the Greek character sketch, and he has a mocking study of the *mempsimoiros*, which is worth quoting in full:

Querulousness is an undue complaining about one's lot; the queru-lous man will say to him that brings him a portion from his friend's table: "You begrudged me your soup or your collops, or you would have asked me to dine with you in person." When his mistress is kissing him he says, "I wonder whether you kiss me so warmly from your heart." He is displeased with Zeus, not because he sends no rain, but because he has been so long about sending it. When he finds a purse in the street, it is: "Ah! but I never found a treasure." When he has bought a slave cheap with much importuning the seller, he cries: "I wonder if my bargain's too cheap to be good." When they bring him the good news that he has a son born to him, then it is: "If you add that I have lost half my fortune, you'll speak the truth." Should this man win a suit-at-law by a unanimous verdict, he is sure to find fault with his speech-writer for omitting so many of the pleas. And if a subscription has been got up for him among his friends, and one of them says to him: "You can cheer up now," he will say: "What? when I must repay each man his share, and be beholden to him into the bargain?"

Here, vividly drawn by Theophrastus's subtle pen, is the picture of a man who can find something to grumble about in any situation. He can find some fault with the best of bargains, the kindest of deeds, the most complete of successes, the richest of good fortune. "There is great gain in godliness with contentment" (1 *Timothy* 6: 6); but the evil men are chronically discontented with life and with the place in life that God has given to them. There are few people more unpopular than chronic grumblers and all such might do well to remember that such grumbling is in its own way an insult to God.

(ii) Jude reiterates a point about these wicked men, which he has made again and again—their conduct is governed by their desires. To them self-discipline and self-control are nothing; to them the moral law is only a burden and a nuisance; honour and duty have no claim upon them; they have no desire to serve and no sense of responsibility. Their one value is pleasure and their one dynamic is desire. If all men were like that, the world would be in complete chaos.

(iii) They speak with pride and arrogance, yet at the same time they are ready to pander to the great, if they think that they can get anything out of it. It is perfectly possible for a man at one and the same time to be a bombastic creature towards the people he wishes to impress and a flattering lick-spittle to the people whom he thinks important. Jude's opponents are glorifiers of themselves and flatterers of others, as they think the occasion demands; and their descendants are sometimes still among us.

THE CHARACTERISTICS OF ERROR (1)

Jude 17–19

But you, beloved, you must remember the words which were once spoken by the apostles of our Lord Jesus Christ; you must remember that they said to us: "In the last time there will be mockers, whose conduct is governed by their own impious desires." These are the people who set up divisions—fleshly creatures, without the Spirit.

JUDE points out to his own people that nothing has happened which they might not have expected. The apostles had given warning that in the last times just such evil men as are now among them would come. The actual words of Jude's quotation are not in any New Testament book. He may be doing any one of three things. He may be quoting some apostolic book which we no longer possess. He may be quoting, not a book, but some oral tradition of the apostolic preaching; or some sermon which he himself had heard from the apostles. He may be giving the general sense of a passage like 1 *Timothy* 4: 1–3. In any event he is telling his people that error was only to be expected in the church. From this passage we can see certain of the characteristics of these evil men.

(i) They mock at goodness and their conduct is governed by their own evil desires. The two things go together. These opponents of Jude had two characteristics, as we have already seen. They believed the body, being matter, was evil; and that, therefore, it made no difference if a man sated its desires. Further, they argued that, since grace could forgive any sin, sin did not matter. These heretics had a third characteristic. They believed that they were the advanced thinkers; and they regarded those who observed the old moral standards as old-fashioned and out of date.

That point of view is by no means dead. There are still those who believe that the once-accepted standards of morality and fidelity, especially in matters of sex, are quite out of date. There is a terrible text in the Old Testament: "The fool says in his heart, There is no God" (*Psalm* 53: 1). In that text *fool* does not mean the brainless man; it means the man who is playing the fool. And the fact that he says there is no God is entirely due to wishful thinking. He knows that, if there is a God, he is wrong and can look for judgment; therefore, he eliminates him. In the last analysis those who eliminate the moral law and give free rein to their passions and desires, do so because they want to do as they like. They listen to themselves instead of listening to God—and they forget that there will come a day when they will be compelled to listen to him.

THE CHARACTERISTICS OF ERROR (2)

Jude 17-19 (*continued*)

(ii) These evil men have a second characteristic. They set up divisions—they are fleshly creatures, without the Spirit. Here is a most significant thought—to set up divisions within the church is always sin. These men set up divisions in two ways.

(*a*) As we have already seen, even at the Love Feasts they had their own little cliques. By their conduct they were steadily destroying fellowship within the church. They were drawing a circle to shut men out instead of drawing a circle to take them in.

(*b*) But they went further. There were certain thinkers in the early church who had a way of looking at human nature which essentially split men into two classes. To understand this we must know something of Greek psychology. To the Greek man was body (*sōma*), soul (*psuchē*) and spirit (*pneuma*). *Sōma* was simply man's physical construction. *Psuchē* is more difficult to understand. To the Greeks *soul*, *psuchē*, was simply *physical life*; everything that lived and breathed had *psuchē*. *Pneuma*, *spirit*, was quite different, it belonged to man alone, and was that which made him a thinking creature, kin to God, able to speak to God and to hear him.

These thinkers went on to argue that all men possessed *psuchē*, but very few really possessed *pneuma*. Only the really intellectual, the élite, possessed *pneuma*; and, therefore, only the very few could rise to real religion. The rest must be content to walk on the lower levels of religious experience.

They, therefore, divided men into two classes. There were the *psuchikoi*, who were physically alive but intellectually and spiritually dead. We might call them *the fleshly creatures*. All they possessed was flesh and blood life; intellectual progress and spiritual experience were beyond them. There were the *pneumatikoi*, who were capable of real intellectual knowledge, real knowledge of God and real spiritual experience. Here was the creation of an intellectual and spiritual aristocracy over against the common herd of men.

Further, these people who believed themselves to be the *pneumatikoi*, believed that they were exempt from all the ordinary laws governing a man's conduct. Ordinary people might have to observe the accepted standards but they were above that. For them sin did not exist; they were so advanced that they could do anything and be none the worse. We may well remember that there are still people who believe that

they are above the laws, who say in their hearts that it could never happen to them and believe that they can get away with anything.

We can now see how cleverly Jude deals with these people who say that the rest of the world are the *psuchikoi*, while they are the *pneumatikoi*. Jude takes their words and reverses them. "It is you," he thunders at them, "who are the *psuchikoi*, the flesh-dominated; it is you who possess no *pneuma*, no real knowledge and no experience of God." Jude is saying to these people that, although they think themselves the only truly religious people, they have no real religion at all. Those whom they despise are, in fact, much better than they are themselves.

The truth about these so-called intellectual and spiritual people was that they desired to sin and twisted religion into a justification for sin.

THE CHARACTERISTICS OF GOODNESS

Jude 20, 21

> But you, beloved, must build yourselves up on the foundation of your most holy faith; you must pray in the Holy Spirit; you must keep yourselves in the love of God; while you wait for the mercy of our Lord Jesus Christ which will bring you to life eternal.

IN the previous passage Jude described the characteristics of error, here he describes the characteristics of goodness.

(i) The good man builds up his life on the foundation of the most holy faith. That is to say, the life of the Christian is founded, not on something which he manufactured himself, but on something which he received. There is a chain in the transmission of the faith. The faith came from Jesus to the apostles; it came from the apostles to the church; and it comes from the church to us. There is something tremendous here. It means that the faith which we hold is not merely someone's personal opinion; it is a revelation which came from Jesus

Christ and was preserved and transmitted within his church, always under the care and the guidance of the Holy Spirit, from generation to generation.

That faith is a *most holy faith*. Again and again we have seen the meaning of this word *holy*. Its root meaning is *different*. That which is *holy* is *different* from other things, as the priest is different from other worshippers, the Temple different from other buildings, the Sabbath different from other days and God supremely different from men.

Our faith is different in two ways. (*a*) It is different from other faiths and from philosophies in that it is not man-made but God-given, not opinion but revelation, not guessing but certainty. (*b*) It is different in that it has the power to make those who believe it different. It is not only a mind-changer but also a life-changer; not only an intellectual belief but also a moral dynamic.

(ii) The good man is a man of prayer. It has been put this way: "Real religion means *dependence*." The essence of religion is the admission of our total dependence on God; and prayer is the acknowledging of that dependence, and the going to God for the help we need. As Moffatt has it in a magnificent definition: "Prayer is love in need appealing to love in power." The Christian must be a man of prayer for at least two reasons. (*a*) He knows that he must test every-thing by the will of God and, therefore, he must take everything to God for his approval. (*b*) He knows that of himself he can do nothing but that with God all things are possible and, therefore, he must ever be taking his in-sufficiency to God's sufficiency.

Prayer, says Jude, is to be *in the Holy Spirit*. What he means is this. Our human prayers are at least sometimes bound to be selfish and blind. It is only when the Holy Spirit takes full possession of us that our desires are so purified that our prayers are right. The truth is that as Christians we are bound to pray to God, but he alone can teach us how to pray and what to pray for.

(iii) The good man keeps himself in the love of God. What

Jude is thinking of here is the old covenant relationship between God and his people as described in *Exodus* 24: 1–8. God came to his people promising that he would be their God and they would be his people; but that relationship depended on their accepting and obeying the law which he gave them. "God's love," Moffatt comments, "has its own terms of communion." It is true in one sense that we can never drift beyond God's love and care; but it is also true that, if we desire to remain in close communion with God, we must give him the perfect love and the perfect obedience which must ever go hand in hand.

(iv) The good man waits with expectation. He waits for the coming of Jesus Christ in mercy, love and power; for he knows that Christ's purpose for him is to bring him to life eternal, which is nothing other than the life of God himself.

RECLAIMING THE LOST

Jude 22, 23

> Some of them you must argue out of their error, while they are still wavering. Others you must rescue by snatching them out of the fire. Others you must pity and fear at the same time, hating the garment stained by the flesh.

DIFFERENT translators give differing translations of this passage. The reason is that there is much doubt as to what the true Greek text is. We have given the translation which we believe to be nearest to the sense of the passage.

Even to the worst heretics, even to those most far gone in error and to those whose beliefs are most dangerous, the Christian has a binding duty not to destroy but to save. His aim must be, not to banish them from the Christian church, but to win them back into the Christian fellowship. James Denney said that, to put the matter at its simplest, Jesus came to make bad men good. Sir John Seeley said: "When the power of reclaiming the lost dies out of the church, it ceases to be the church." As we have taken this passage, Jude divides the troublers of the church into three classes, to each of whom a different approach is necessary.

(i) There are those who are flirting with falsehood. They are obviously attracted by the wrong way and are on the brink of committing themselves to error, but are still hesitating before taking the final step. They must be argued out of their error while there is time. From this two things emerge as a duty.

(a) We must study to be able to defend the faith and to give a reason for the hope that is in us. We must know what we believe so that we can meet error with truth; and we must make ourselves able to defend the faith in such a way that our graciousness and sincerity may win others to it. To do this we must banish all uncertainty from our minds and all arrogance and intolerance from our approach to others.

(b) We must be ready to speak in time. Many a person would have been saved from error of thought and of action, if someone else had only spoken in time. Sometimes we hesitate to speak, but there are many times when silence is cowardly and can cause more harm than speech could ever cause. One of the greatest tragedies in life is when someone comes to us and says, "I would never have been in the mess I am now in, if someone—you, perhaps—had only spoken to me."

(ii) There are those who have to be snatched from the fire. They have actually started out on the wrong way and have to be stopped, as it were, forcibly, and even against their will. It is all very well to say that we must leave a man his freedom and that he has a right to do what he likes. All these things are in one sense true, but there are times when a man must be even forcibly saved from himself.

(iii) There are those whom we must pity and fear at one and the same time. Here Jude is thinking of something which is always true. There is danger to the sinner; but there is also danger to the rescuer. He who would cure an infectious disease runs the risk of infection. Jude says that we must hate the garment stained by the flesh. Almost certainly he is thinking here of the regulations in *Leviticus* 13: 47–52, where it is laid down that the garment worn by a person discovered to be suffering from leprosy must be burned. The old saying remains true—we must love the sinner but hate the sin. Before a man can rescue others, he must himself be strong in the faith. His own feet must be firm on the dry land before he can throw a lifebelt to the man who is likely to be swept away. The simple fact is that the rescue of those in error is not for everyone to attempt. Those who would win others for Christ must themselves be very sure of him; and those who would fight the disease of sin must themselves have the strong anti-septic of a healthy faith. Ignorance can never be met with ignorance, nor even with partial knowledge; it can be met only by the affirmation, "I know whom I have believed."

THE FINAL ASCRIPTION OF PRAISE

Jude 24, 25

Unto him who is able to keep you from slipping and to make you stand blameless and exultant in the presence of his glory, to the only God, our Saviour, through Jesus Christ our Lord, be glory, majesty, dominion and power, before all time, at this present time, and for all time. Amen.

Jude comes to an end with a tremendous ascription of praise.

Three times in the New Testament praise is given to *the God who is able*. In *Romans* 16: 25 Paul gives praise to the God who is able to strengthen us. God is the one person who can give us a foundation for life which nothing and no one can ever shake. In *Ephesians* 3: 20 Paul gives praise to the God who is able to do far more than we can ever ask or even dream of. He is the God whose grace no man has every exhausted and on whom no claim can ever be too much.

Here Jude offers *his* praise to the God who is able.

(i) God is able to keep us from slipping. The word is *aptaistos*. It is used both of a sure-footed horse which does not stumble and of a man who does not fall into error. "He will not let your foot be moved," or as the Scottish metrical version has it, "Thy foot he'll not let slide" (*Psalm* 121: 3). To walk with God is to walk in safety even on the most dangerous and the most slippery path. In mountaineering climbers are roped together so that even if the inexperienced climber should slip, the skilled mountaineer can take his weight and save him. Even so, when we bind ourselves to God, he keeps us safe.

(ii) He can make us stand blameless in the presence of his glory. The word for blameless is *amōmos*. This is characteristically a sacrificial word; and it is commonly and technically used of an animal which is without spot or blemish and is therefore fit to be offered to God. The amazing thing is that when we submit ourselves to God, his grace can make our lives nothing less than a sacrifice fit to offer to him.

(iii) He can bring us into his presence exultant. Surely the natural way to think of entry into the presence of God is in fear and in shame. But by the work of Jesus Christ and in the grace of God, we know that we can go to God with joy and with all fear banished. Through Jesus Christ, God the stern Judge has become known to us as God the loving Father.

We note one last thing. Usually we associate the word *Saviour* with Jesus Christ, but here Jude attaches it to God. He is not alone in this, for God is often called Saviour in the New Testament (*Luke* 1: 47; 1 *Timothy* 1: 1; 2: 3; 4: 10; *Titus* 1: 3; 2: 10; 3: 4). So we end with the great and comforting certainty that at the back of everything there is a God whose name is Saviour. The Christian has the joyous certainty that in this world he lives in the love of God and that in the next world he goes to that love. The love of God is at once the atmosphere and the goal of all his living.

FURTHER READING

John

J. N. S. Alexander, *The Epistles of John* (Tch; *E*)
A. E. Brooke, *The Johannine Epistles* (ICC; *G*)
C. H. Dodd, *The Johannine Epistles* (MC; *E*)

Jude

C. Bigg, *St Peter and St Jude* (ICC; *G*)
C. E. B. Cranfield, *1 and 2 Peter and Jude* (Tch; *E*)
J. B. Mayor, *The Second Epistle of St Peter and the Epistle of St Jude* (MmC; *G*)
J. Moffatt, *The General Epistles: James, Peter and Jude* (MC; *E*)

Abbreviations

ICC : International Critical Commentary
MC : Moffatt Commentary
MmC: Macmillan Commentary
Tch : Torch Commentary

E : English Text
G : Greek Text

THE DAILY STUDY BIBLE

Published in 17 Volumes